the stop walking on eggshells

WORKBOOK

SECOND EDITION

PRACTICAL STRATEGIES FOR

LIVING WITH SOMEONE WHO HAS

BORDERLINE PERSONALITY DISORDER

RANDI KREGER

New Harbinger Publications, Inc.

Publisher's Note

This publication is designed to provide accurate and authoritative information in regard to the subject matter covered. It is sold with the understanding that the publisher is not engaged in rendering psychological, financial, legal, or other professional services. If expert assistance or counseling is needed, the services of a competent professional should be sought.

NEW HARBINGER PUBLICATIONS is a registered trademark of New Harbinger Publications, Inc.

New Harbinger Publications is an employee-owned company.

Quotations from *I'm Not Supposed to Be Here* by Rachel Reiland are reprinted with her permission. Published by Eggshells Press, 2002.

Quotations and recommendations from Teresa Whitehurst are printed with her permission.

Cover design by Amy Shoup

Acquired by Georgia Kolias

Edited by Max Sylvia

Library of Congress Cataloging-in-Publication Data on file

Printed in the United States of America

28   27   26

10 9 8 7 6 5 4 3 2 1   First Printing

This workbook was developed to be used with my other books, including *Stop Walking on Eggshells,* *Stop Walking on Eggshells for Parents,* and *Stop Walking on Eggshells for Partners.* If you are a parent or a partner, I strongly advise that you obtain a copy of the book written for you that takes on your hardest challenges. My fifth book, *The Essential Family Guide to Borderline Personality Disorder,* teaches readers five tools to manage a relationship with someone who has BPD. I recommend that book to everyone who shares their life with someone who has borderline personality disorder.

Contents

Preface to the Second Edition

I'll confess to it now: In 1996, I sneaked into BookExpo America at the vast McCormick Place in Chicago to pitch what was to become *Stop Walking on Eggshells*, my first book. My goal was to talk to the publishers that had received my book proposal but had not yet replied. A year of talking to family members and loved ones online made me feel a moral imperative: My readers were desperate for the information in the book. And simple math demonstrated I had an enormous audience. When I took the population of individuals with borderline personality disorder and multiplied it by four or five (the rough number of family members related to each individual), I came up with a potential readership of at least thirty-five million. The number of books available on my topic was zero. The challenge was finding a publisher smart enough to pounce on what I thought was a golden opportunity. I had already received about thirty rejections.

As my husband followed me around carrying copies of the proposal in a large backpack, I ignored the circus-like atmosphere of the place with the hope of talking to as many acquisitions editors as I could. I had a lot to communicate in three to five minutes; the amount of time I figured busy acquisitions editors were likely to give me. Borderline personality disorder is a notoriously difficult mental health issue to understand. I had my work cut out for me.

In general, it wasn't a receptive audience. One publisher's booth featured Fabio, a blond model for countless romance novels. The hallway was chock full of giggling women who wanted to get their picture taken with him, and an editor I tried to talk with had her eyes on him the whole time. One man talked to me for thirty minutes before confessing that he wasn't interested in publishing the book; he was looking for advice for his brother, who had a wife with BPD. An editor from a psychiatric publisher dismissed me right away because I didn't use the psychological terminology she preferred. One editor said there weren't enough books like it to publish mine. Another one told me the market was flooded with books like mine.

Finally, I arrived at one of the smallest booths, New Harbinger Publications. Standing there was the co-founder of the publishing company himself, Matt McKay, a psychologist, who had begun the business to provide self-help books that offered "real tools for real change." For once, I did not have to define BPD. That left me time to explain why my book would be both a bestseller and a blessing. And Matt got it. He said "yes." And I kept my promise—*Stop Walking on Eggshells* did become a bestseller, with over a million copies sold in seventeen languages.

Over the past twenty-eight years, New Harbinger and I have worked together to provide people with a borderline or narcissistic loved one with several desperately needed books and other materials, including *Stop Walking on Eggshells for Parents, Stop Walking on Eggshells for Partners,* and the *Stop Walking on Eggshells Card Deck.* Along the way, I revised the original book—twice. What I appreciate is that New Harbinger trusts me to know my audience and the subject matter, and I trust them in return. Thank you for enabling me to follow my dream of giving the loved ones of high-conflict people a voice.

Since 1996, I have listened to the stories of literally thousands of people who have a loved one with borderline personality disorder (BPD) or narcissistic personality disorder (NPD). I've learned about the varying needs of spouses, romantic partners, siblings, grandparents, adult and adolescent children, children-in-law, parents-in-law, and parents of individuals with personality disorders. They have been my teachers, explaining the problems they face, the questions they want answers to, and the no-win situations that made them feel trapped. My readers have given me the motivation to hang on and keep going all these years, urging me to keep at it even during difficult times.

I never meant to write books for a living. I was happy doing marketing and public relations. But this job chose me, and it turned out I had been preparing for it all my life. Not everyone finds their true purpose in life, and I did. A big thank you to those who made it possible.

CHAPTER 1

Does Someone in Your Life Have Traits of Borderline or Narcissistic Personality Disorder?

I feel like I've been forced to drink three shots, put through the spin cycle of a washing machine, and asked to play Pin the Tail on the Donkey. And if I don't put the tail in the right place, God help me.

—A member of the Moving Forward online support community

You're probably reading this workbook because you or your therapist suspect that someone in your life has borderline personality disorder (BPD) or narcissistic personality disorder (NPD). Or perhaps the title struck a chord. It's possible that a friend or therapist recommended it, or that you've read one of my four other books on personality disorders: *Stop Walking on Eggshells, Stop Walking on Eggshells for Parents, Stop Walking on Eggshells for Partners,* or *The Essential Family Guide to Borderline Personality Disorder.*

Whatever the circumstances, it's likely that a current or past relationship is causing you pain. The person who is the source of this grief may be alive and part of your everyday life. Or they could be a long-deceased parent. You may not understand who or what is responsible for the distress, let alone what to do about it. You may not even be able to describe how it has affected you. But like the main character in *The Matrix,* you sense that something is wrong and has been for a long time.

How Do You Feel Right Now?

Do you feel isolated, distrustful, and flawed? Do you live in fear of disagreements, unable to do anything but wait for the other shoe to drop—or fly across the room? Do you feel trapped and helpless, unable to leave or stay in an important but unhealthy relationship?

You may be one of 60 million people in the United States and Canada (millions more live overseas) whose life is being affected by a person who has borderline personality disorder or narcissistic personality disorder. These traits of disordered thinking, emoting, and acting have names and diagnoses. And you can take action to improve your situation whether or not you continue to have a relationship.

This book will refer to an individual with traits of BPD and NPD as a "high-conflict person" (HCP). I define an HCP as someone who may have BPD, NPD, or traits of either disorder. Throughout the book, I will also refer to "non-HCPs," meaning someone who is not a high-conflict person.

As you use this workbook, you'll find Action Steps that include exercises and reflection questions. You may want to keep a dedicated notebook to complete these exercises and have space to fully respond to open-ended questions.

One way to tell if someone you care about has BPD or NPD is to pay attention to how you experience the relationship and how it makes you feel. People who love someone with BPD or NPD often say "yes" to the following questions.

Action Step: Identify the Problem

Below are statements you may identify with. On a scale of 1–5, with 5 being high, write down the number of the intensity of your feelings and experiences.

A. _____ Do you find yourself hiding negative thoughts or feelings because it's easier than dealing with the other person's overreactions or because talking about problems simply makes them worse?

B. _____ After you try to explain yourself to the other person they use your own words and contort them to prove their own point (usually that you are "bad" or doing something wrong)? Does this person blame you for all the problems in the relationship and refuse to acknowledge that their own actions cause problems for other people and themselves?

C. _____ Is their temper so unpredictable that you're constantly on your toes, adrenaline pumping, waiting for the next verbal attack? When you try to calm them down, does it only make them angrier? Is it difficult to enjoy the good times because you've been sucked in too often and you've learned to never let your guard down?

D. _____ Do you feel as if your loved one sees you as either all good or all bad, with nothing in between? Is there sometimes no rational reason for the switch? Do you wonder which version of your loved one you'll be interacting with day to day? Will they be the person who cares for you or the petty tyrant whose energy supply seems to come from intense, violent, and irrational rages? Does no one believe you when you explain that this is going on because it only happens in private?

E. _____ Do you feel manipulated, controlled, or even lied to sometimes? Does your loved one attempt to get what they want by making you responsible for their feelings (gaslighting and emotional blackmail). For example, "If you don't let me go to the rock concert, I swear I'll hate you for the rest of my life," or, "Only an ungrateful and selfish daughter would rather stay at school for Christmas instead of coming home."

F. _____ Does the person seem to demand constant attention? Is everything always about them?

G. _____ Are you afraid to ask for things from them because you will be told that you're selfish and demanding?

H. _____ Does your loved one imply, explicitly declare, or show by example that your needs are not as important as theirs are?

I. _____ Do they continually contradict your needs and opinions so they can be the voice of authority?

J. _____ Do you feel that their expectations of you are constantly changing so you can never do anything right?

K. _____ Are you accused of doing things you never did and saying things you never said?

L. _____ Do you feel misunderstood, and when you try to explain, do you find that they don't believe you?

M. _____ Do you feel emotionally, verbally, or physically abused?

N. _____ Do other people remark that your loved one is verbally and emotionally abusive or encourage you to reduce the amount of time you give to the relationship, or to go completely no contact? (No contact means exactly what it says.)

O. _____ If you try to leave, do they attempt to prevent you from departing by trying to convince you that no one else loves you more or could put up with someone like you? Or do they promise to change (and then don't or can't keep it up)?

P. _____ Do you have a hard time planning social engagements, vacations, and other activities because your loved one's moodiness, impulsiveness, or unpredictability destroys your plans at the last minute?

Q. _____ Do you make excuses for their behavior to convince others (and yourself) that this is okay?

R. _____ Right now, are you thinking, "I had no idea that anyone else was going through this?"

Action Step: Tell Your Story

Now, we'll take a closer look at how this is affecting your life. This is an important part of your recovery. I've included examples below to help you. As with all the examples in this book, the stories are real, but I have changed many details to conceal the authors' identities. After each example, write your own story. You don't have to write the entire story, just enough to jog your memory.

Do you find yourself hiding negative thoughts or feelings?

Gail's response: *During the years, I've learned not to contradict my mother when she's in one of her moods—especially when she's been drinking, too. She gets argumentative over nothing and tries to pound it into my head. I don't say anything because whatever I say will be wrong. If she asks me a question, I just say, "I don't know." Even though I'm thirty-three, I remember the day I discovered I could just say "I don't know" (I was only eleven), and sometimes that worked to shut her up. At the time, I thought all mothers acted that way.*

_____

_____

_____

_____

_____

_____

_____

After you try to explain yourself to your loved one, do they use your own words and contort them to prove their own point (usually that you are "bad" or doing something wrong)? Do they refuse to acknowledge that their own actions cause problems for other people and themselves?

Rochelle's response: *I drove out to Georgia to visit my sister-in-law, nieces, and my brother, who has BPD. It's been a long time since I've seen him because of his behavior, but since I was going in that direction I figured I might as well stop by. So when I brought up the fact that we hadn't spoken in a long time, he started yelling at me that I never cared about him, that our parents loved me more—which I don't think is true, except that he caused them a lot of grief. He kept going on and I couldn't go anywhere because we were in the car.*

_____

_____

_____

_____

_____

_____

_____

_____

Is their temper so unpredictable that you're constantly on your toes, adrenaline pumping, waiting for the next verbal attack? Is it difficult to enjoy the good times because you've learned not to let down your guard?

Bill's response: *Our son is sixteen, so sometimes it's hard to see where BPD behavior and typical teen behavior start and stop. Since he won't go to therapy, it probably doesn't matter. We live our lives in fear. We sleep in our clothes with our car keys under the pillow in case we need to get out of the house ASAP because of his physical threats. Every time the phone rings late at night, we expect it to be the hospital. When the door rings unexpectedly, our automatic thought is,* He's overdosed, gotten in a car wreck, shoplifted, whatever—*and it's the police.*

His therapy has cost us thousands of dollars—money we could have used to send our daughter to college. We have no idea how she has been affected by this and, frankly, we're afraid to dig deep. We are counting the days until he is eighteen and we are no longer legally responsible for his actions. We love him, but we've learned that love is not enough.

_____

_____

_____

_____

_____

_____

_____

_____

Do you feel like your loved one sees you as either all good or all bad, with nothing in between? Is there sometimes no rational reason for the switch? Do you wonder which version of your loved one you'll be interacting with day to day? Will they be the person who cares for you or the petty tyrant whose energy supply seems to come from intense, violent, and irrational rages?

Susan's response: *My partner, Joan, and I have a small public relations agency. We were so excited when we landed a major project for a mortgage insurance (MI) agency—promoting an incentive program for the loan processors who often make the decision as to which MI company to use. We knew we needed help, so we asked my ad agency friend Rob if he would help us out on a freelance, hourly basis. Rob, Joan, and I generated a lot of ideas and ended up with an incentive program that the client really loved. The trouble began when Joan and I, as owners of the agency, flew down to make the presentation. Rob felt slighted and complained loudly, claiming that we should have paid to fly him, too. Then he wanted an office and computer. It seemed like our original agreement went out the window. When I told him no, he started screaming that he was unappreciated and that we had just "used" him, accusing us of only caring about the money and not the client. After he stormed out, I had no idea what to do. I had never thought to ask Rob to sign a non-compete clause, so he went directly to the MI company and told them that he had designed the entire program! And they believed him! We later learned that he had narcissistic personality disorder as well as BPD.*

_____

_____

_____

_____

_____

_____

_____

_____

Do you feel manipulated, controlled, or even lied to sometimes? Does your loved one attempt to get what they want by making you responsible for their feelings (e.g., "If you don't let me go to the rock concert I swear I'll hate you for the rest of my life" or, "Only an ungrateful and selfish daughter would rather stay at school for Christmas instead of coming home."

Sarah's response: *To outsiders, my mother appears to be a highly educated college professor. But my life was a never-ending nightmare of her manipulation, control, and abuse. I was never allowed to express anger to my mother, question or disobey her, and was punished severely whenever I broke these rules. At age fifteen, I awoke to go to school only to discover that my makeup and contact lenses were missing. My mother refused to return them to me until I "apologized" for something I had said the night before. At seventeen, I refused to do some household chores because I had to study for an exam the following day (I was a straight-A, honor student). My mother flew into a rage and slapped me. My mother falsely informed the students in the college course she was teaching that my boyfriend had raped me and given me a venereal disease—I learned this later from one of the students in that class. When I refused to run an errand for her, she dumped an extremely expensive bottle of my perfume in the toilet.*

When I told her I had discussed marriage with my now-husband, and that he didn't feel ready, she called him at work and told him I was suicidal because he didn't want to marry me. When my father gave her just three presents at Christmas a few years ago (they had agreed to spend less money), she cornered me and went into a hysterical sobbing fit about how cruel he was. She stated that she wasn't going to say anything, though, because she didn't want to ruin anyone's Christmas (except mine, I guess).

_____

_____

_____

_____

_____

_____

_____

Does the person demand constant attention? Is everything always about them? For example, when your loved one attends an event that is celebrating someone else, will they create a scene that will bring the attention back to them?

Andy's response: *Sometimes I can't believe how self-centered my wife is. When I had to get a biopsy, she complained because we had to cancel a Halloween party. Then, when my father died and I had to leave suddenly for his funeral, she complained that I was leaving "so suddenly" and that I was leaving her alone. If I mentioned this to anyone, I don't know if they'd believe me.*

_____

_____

_____

_____

_____

_____

_____

_____

Are you afraid to ask for things in the relationship because your family member will tell you you're selfish and demanding? Does your loved one imply, explicitly declare, or show by example that your needs are not as important as theirs?

Marcia's response: *Since our son got married to a woman (Nell) whom I suspect has BPD, she has done all she can to alienate us from him. Once Nell and my husband had an argument about something—I think it was a last-minute babysitting job. Although we wanted very much to see our grandson, we just couldn't take care of him right then because we had plans.*

My husband finally got fed up with feeling manipulated and said no, and Nell screamed at him and slammed down the phone. Now she won't "let" my son or grandson visit us. We feel like we've lost our son and grandchild, and the pain is unbearable. We don't know what to do. My son just seems mesmerized by her and isn't willing to take a stand.

_____

_____

_____

_____

_____

_____

_____

_____

Does this person continually contradict your needs and opinions so they can be the voice of authority? Do you feel that their expectations of you are constantly changing, so you can never do anything right?

Linda's response: *I am always in a no-win situation with my borderline husband. If I take the kids to lessons and soccer, I am ignoring him and pressuring the kids. If I don't, I'm accused of not "offering them enough experiences." If I call him at his home office, I am intruding. If I don't, he says I must not love him. If I get him a present, he always exchanges it. If I don't, I'm self-absorbed and "don't care." We make decisions and he gets mad when I do what we said I would do. I can't take much more of this.*

_____

_____

_____

_____

_____

_____

_____

_____

Are you accused of doing things you never did and saying things you never said? Do you feel misunderstood, and when you try to explain, do you find that they don't believe you?

Kwan's response: *My mother was coming to San Francisco to visit me. We were talking about me taking off work when I reminded her that I was working "summer hours" and already had Friday afternoon off. Suddenly she started screaming uncontrollably and hung up on me. I tried to call back, and she did the same thing. Finally, I found out she was interpreting my statement about summer hours to mean "That's all I'm going to take off." I didn't say that and I didn't mean that, but she refused to let me explain.*

_____

_____

_____

_____

_____

_____

_____

_____

Do other people, including your therapist, remark that your loved one is verbally and emotionally abusive or encourage you to limit or avoid contact with them? But if you do try to leave, does the other person attempt to prevent you from leaving by trying to convince you no one else loves you or could put up with someone like you?

Harry's response: *My girlfriend goes through a pattern you can set a clock by. First comes the "I love you" part where everything is wonderful. That's what keeps me in the relationship. Then comes the "you're crowding me" speech and the tension builds until she says she wants to break up. We do. Then three days later she calls as though nothing had happened. I have never seen this kind of behavior before. When things are good, they're great. But why does this cycle keep happening?*

_____

_____

_____

_____

_____

_____

_____

_____

Now I'm going to switch from your feelings to the traits of BPD and NPD.

What Is a Personality Disorder?

A personality disorder is a pattern of inner experience and behavior that differs markedly from the person's culture. These patterns are inflexible and pervasive across many situations and cause significant distress, especially for their loved ones.

In recent years, research says that 40% of people with BPD have narcissistic personality disorder and vice versa (2008, Grant et al). We didn't know this until 2008, when a group of researchers decided to go out into the wider community to determine the prevalence of BPD and the percentage of people with co-occurring disorders. Previously, researchers had only used subjects in treatment health-care settings.

But one of the critical reasons why someone with BPD would refuse to see a physician is co-occurring NPD. Thus, I will go over both personality disorders. Your loved one may have the full-blown disorders, or just traits of them. It is essential that you understand which personality disorder(s) your they may have because once you have a working theory that they have BPD, NPD, or both, you can better predict their behavior, understand what's behind it, and develop the right skills. In my experience, a well-read friend, family member, or loved one can more accurately identify BPD or NPD than an average mental health professional.

Traits Unique to Borderline Personality Disorder (BPD)

Next, I will discuss the key differences between the disorders beginning with BPD. In the next chapter, I will go over the similarities between BPD and NPD. Get a highlighter and highlight the traits that are familiar to you. Use one color for BPD and another for NPD.

Fear of Abandonment

Fear of abandonment, a hallmark symptom of BPD, shows itself in a multitude of ways:

- Exaggerated reactions when you are late, spend time with someone else, or prioritize your own needs

- Threats to leave you (they reject you before you can reject them)

- Demands that you be immediately accessible to them, such as expecting you to respond to their numerous texts within minutes

- Statements such as, "You love them more than me," or "You've never loved me," or "You'll do this if you love me"

- Constant jealousy, not only of other potential romantic interests but also of your family, friends, and even pets

- Stringing out the divorce process so they still have contact with you, even if it's negative

- Stalking you online or in real life after a breakup

People with this disorder seesaw from fears of abandonment to fears of engulfment, which is feeling submerged in a relationship. Sometimes they push you away, and other times they pull you in. For example, the morning after a wonderful night of lovemaking, they tear into you because you left your clothes all over the floor.

Trying to use logic to convince your loved one that you are not abandoning them is usually fruitless because fear exists in the limbic system (the "emotional brain") and not the prefrontal cortex (the "thinking brain"). They easily ignore facts when they differ from their feelings. For people with BPD, their feelings equal facts.

Impulsive "Pain Management" Behaviors

To know what it's like to have BPD, imagine a world in which you are positively sure that you are a complete and utter failure, and everyone thinks you're an idiot, aren't worth listening to, and can't be trusted. When you get a chance to show them differently, it turns out wrong no matter what you do. So, you wrap yourself in self-loathing.

—**Ruth**

The combination of your loved one's exquisite sensitivity, all-or-nothing thinking, and feelings of shame and worthlessness means that they are constantly in emotional pain—even if you don't see it. When something happens to trigger them (and it could just be a thought), they're looking for comfort immediately. They impulsively try to manage their pain by doing things like shoplifting, binge eating, acting recklessly, and spending too much. Some people with BPD self-harm or have suicidal thoughts. But as I said earlier, people with BPD depend on others to manage their emotions. Making you the target of blame is a pain-management measure.

People with BPD think negative thoughts about themselves, their world, and their future much more often than the average person. This rumination increases the severity of their symptoms and leads to an "emotional cascade" that leads to more impulsive pain management behaviors (Selby and Joiner 2009).

Difficulty with Empathy

My borderline wife has difficulty recognizing the needs and feelings of others. She is oblivious to the way I hurt when she says mean things to me or acts like she doesn't care. I have always had empathy for her, especially knowing her background, but I don't feel it coming back in the other direction. Doesn't she realize that I need to be comforted too?

—Stephan

When people with BPD are in a highly emotional state, they're not aware of how their behavior is affecting you, or they are indifferent to it. Again, feelings equal facts. Remember they're almost always in emotional overload, encumbered by negative painful feelings. Their problem is not so much a lack of empathy as much as an inability to set aside their own intense emotions and focus on yours. Some self-aware people with BPD deeply regret it when they've hurt someone. They feel shame and guilt and apologize. But unfortunately, most don't. If they acknowledge making a mistake, their low self-worth and shame would make them feel even worse.

Severe Mood Swings

How my wife's mind works is a mystery. For example, we were having a great time in the car. It was day one of our three-day getaway. One minute we were chatting about our daughter, and then suddenly she asked me to never talk to my brother's wife again. She thinks my sister-in-law doesn't like her. I hesitated and tried to think of an answer that wouldn't cause her to blow her top. My hesitation was all she needed. She pulled over, yelled that I didn't love her, and began punching and kicking me.

—Jamie

People with BPD tend to have extreme mood swings. One minute everything is fine, and then there is a sudden and intense mood change. Borderline emotions have the following qualities:

Extremely intense. What might make you feel depressed and in need of some chocolate ice cream may strike someone with BPD as a personal tragedy. If most people's emotional range is from one to ten, people with BPD go from minus-twenty to plus-twenty.

Mostly negative. Their mostly negative emotions come from their feelings of shame and worthlessness, along with the expectation that bad things will happen to them, including rejection and being abandoned. When they feel like a mess, they think something is wrong with you because you chose them.

Last a long or short time. Once emotionally aroused, your BPD loved one usually takes a longer time to come back to baseline. You might be feeling better a day after a significant argument, but they might need a week. Or the opposite can happen. Once they feel better, they are surprised that you are still hurting from an argument. Then again, sometimes they will act as if the fight never existed and want something you're in no mood to give.

Swing widely and often. People with BPD are hypersensitive and triggered by things you would consider small. Many of their mood swings won't make any sense to you. But they are very real to your loved one.

Take away from their ability to concentrate or be logical. Rumination, or thinking "attentively, repetitively, or frequently about the self and one's world," can take over the life of people with BPD. Rumination is a drain of mental energy that can take up so much space in your loved one's mind that they have less room for concentration, memory, and problem-solving (Whitbourne 2021).

Feelings of Emptiness and a Lack of Identity

For me, having feelings of emptiness is like having a piano on my chest and stomach, and I'm overcome with loneliness, boredom, and apathy. There's a big piece of me missing. I'm desperate for something that'll take up my time, make me forget about it, and make it go away. I try to fill it up with relationships, but then I end up driving people away. Someone once said that it's due to a lack of a solid sense of self, and I would agree. I don't know who I am as a person, and I don't feel like I have any real identity.

—**Brad**

Feelings of emptiness and a lack of identity are hard to explain to someone who's never felt them. Nothing on the outside of the person may look different. They may go to work, see friends, and so on, but for them, none of it fills in what is missing. It adds to their pain and the likelihood of pain-management behaviors. The emptiness is related to a lack of identity or sense of self.

Brief Stress-Related Paranoia

My wife and I broke up. I told her the day and time I was going to come over and pick up my things so she could arrange to be elsewhere. At the arranged time, I entered the house with my keys and went to the basement. The next thing I knew, my wife was screaming and calling the police because she thought a stranger was coming in to rape her. I am lucky I wasn't arrested.

—**Danny**

People with BPD find it difficult to trust others. This is magnified under stressful situations, such as being criticized, facing real or perceived abandonment, or under the influence of alcohol or other drugs (including prescription drugs, such as stimulants and antidepressants). During these times, they can become especially jealous, suspicious, and worried about other people's motives. It's even more difficult for them to think rationally. They may believe that others are plotting against them or want to hurt them. These episodes can last for hours, days, or even longer.

Differences Between Men and Women

A study shows that half of the people with BPD are men, despite the stereotype that it affects mostly women (Grant et al. 2008). The following attributes are more common in men with BPD than in women with the disorder:

- substance abuse

- unstable relationships

- impulsivity

- aggression (even after controlling for differing levels of the trait by gender)

- co-occurring narcissistic personality disorder

- co-occurring antisocial personality disorder

The following attributes are more common in women with BPD than in men with the disorder:

- a history of being in therapy

- eating disorders

- anxiety disorders

- PTSD

- a major mood disorder, such as depression or bipolar disorder

- taking medication for a mental disorder (Mason and Kreger 2020)

Traits Unique to Narcissistic Personality Disorder (NPD)

The following list of traits are the major characteristics of people with NPD only. If your loved one demonstrates the following traits, they may have NPD or traits of NPD.

Narcissistic Supply

People with NPD rely on others to continually supply self-esteem in the same way that people with BPD need emotional reassurance. They find people who will provide them with that self-esteem in the form of "narcissistic supply." Examples of narcissistic supply include admiration, praise, attention, being envied, having an impressive title, owning expensive things, special treatment, adulation, being feared, approval, affirmation, respect, applause, celebrity status, sexual conquest, notoriety, or any other means of being viewed as the "top dog." (*Stop Walking on Eggshells for Partners*, 2024).

To the person with NPD, their loved one's primary function is to provide a constant flow of narcissistic supply. They expect you to agree with their fantasies of being the latest, the greatest, and the best at everything. If you don't give them as much supply as they need because you have your own life to lead, or if you "betray" them by having your own ideas and opinions, your loved one may call you selfish, castigate you, or complain you're not giving enough.

Narcissistic Injuries

A narcissist injury refers to the emotional pain or distress when someone calls into question the exalted position that the person with NPD imagines to be their real self. It doesn't matter how small the slight is. At the same time, they will injure others without impunity to cover up for their shame and low self-esteem. Examples include being passed over for a promotion, being criticized (even mildly so), or perceived disrespect. These events threaten their fragile ego.

Reactions to narcissistic injuries can be severely overblown. They can occur for reasons that are petty such as not getting the best table at a restaurant or giant, like being edged out as the CEO of a Fortune 500 company, losing an election, or a having a spouse ask for a divorce. They find someone or something else to blame, even if it's only fate. They, of course, are innocent victims in need of sympathy (more supply).

Lack of Empathy

I can't empathize with anyone. I don't care about other people's feelings. I only care about myself. I developed NPD so early in life that I never had the chance to develop a conscience or the capacity to feel remorse or empathy for the way I treat others.

—**Carlos**

While people with BPD have trouble feeling empathy when emotionally aroused, those with NPD completely lack it. They understand it intellectually and they can fake it, but the feeling itself bewilders them. They are bored when you're talking about your bad day. They get irritated when something great happens to you because they're jealous of your good fortune. When something terrible happens to you, all they care about is how your grief is going to affect them. This inability to empathize, or even sympathize, is often the reason why most people with NPD can't sustain successful relationships.

Feelings of Superiority, Self-Importance, and Entitlement

Her sense of entitlement would show up in small and big things. For example, she would demand that I bring her coffee at random points in the day. But she doesn't even remember how I like my tea made.

—**Chris**

People with NPD may latch onto superficial notions of superiority, such as a designer clothing brand or a luxury car, to set them apart from others. They have an exaggerated sense of their accomplishments and will brag in an arrogant way to anyone who will listen. They pay special attention to their grooming, seem to have a high opinion of themselves, and are unwilling to listen to others, especially if those people are marginalized, underprivileged, or have feelings of inferiority, insecurity, or inadequacy. They feel, act, and think that they are entitled to the best of everything, and the rules are made for other people, not them.

Interpersonal Exploitive Behavior

People with NPD treat others as tools for fulfilling their own needs while ignoring the needs of other people. Their relationships with others are often transactional: You scratch my back and I'll scratch yours. They demand to have things done for them, and if you refuse they may use emotional blackmail to get what they want.

The Need to Win at All Costs

While your goals may be to find a win-win solution to problems, minimize conflict, and increase intimacy, your loved one just wants to be right. Being wrong confirms the low self-esteem that lurks under their skin, hidden from sight.

One self-aware person with NPD says, "I get incredibly defensive whenever there is anything I perceive as criticism. I make everything about me. And when someone tells me I have hurt their feelings, I will try to turn it around to show that they are the ones who actually hurt me. Even if I say I'm sorry, it is not sincere."

The First Commandment: Don't Tell Your Loved One You Think They Have a Disorder

When people first find out their loved one may have BPD or NPD, they become excited because it explains so much. I call this the "light bulb effect." It seems like it would be so easy: Just tell your family member what you've learned about these disorders and they will understand that their feelings, thoughts, and actions are distorted and try to change them because they love you.

That is a fantasy that won't end well if your loved one is not in a position to listen and take responsibility for their actions. But that's all it is, a fantasy. When you call out a person with NPD on their manipulation and exploitation, they deny, attack, and reverse victim and offender (DARVO). You will hear, "I'm not the one with the personality disorder. You are!" along with some emotional or verbal abuse. For people with NPD, suggesting that they have a disorder is a major narcissistic injury (when their narcissistic supply of admiration and attention are taken away).

If you criticize someone with BPD (which includes people telling them they have a mental disorder) they may immediately think you're going to abandon them and DARVO as well, but generally will not want to hurt you the same way someone with NPD would.

The exception to this rule of not speaking of it is a case in which they are in therapy and *if* they believe they have a problem and want to work on it, possibly by seeing a therapist, then you can mention what you have learned about BPD and NPD. If they're looking for answers to why they think, feel, and act so differently than most people, and you're sure, then you can risk this—but be prepared for DARVO if that's how they respond. Ideally, their therapist will go over the diagnosis. But if they won't go to therapy (or quit when they don't like what the therapist says), or the therapist believes in concealing their BPD diagnosis (in my opinion a terrible idea) the best way to discuss this is to suggest a couple of different diagnoses or leave materials where they will see them. Let them tell you if they see a match.

If your child has BPD or NPD, especially if they're a minor, I strongly suggest you look up the pros and cons of disclosing the diagnosis to your child in my book *Stop Walking on Eggshells for Parents*.

Types of BPD

BPD is an unusual personality disorder because people who have it can appear completely different from one another—even diametrically opposed. Over the decades, researchers have tried to tease out these differences and develop names for each type. Different researchers have come up with their own findings, and currently, there is no consensus on the subcategories of BPD.

However, in my own twenty-five years of research, I have come up with terms for what seem to be the two basic types: the "conventional" type and the "unconventional" type. There is also a large gray area in the middle.

The Conventional Type

I call this subgroup the "conventional" type because people in this group meet the stereotype of the "typical" person with BPD described in books, on the internet, and so on. If you remember, these folks are only studied within the mental health community. The major criterion of this group is that they self-identify as having BPD and are working hard to overcome the disorder. Aspects of the disorder (like self-harm, suicidal thinking, suicide attempts, and co-occurring disorders, such as bipolar and eating disorders) bring these individuals into inpatient and outpatient mental health settings. They often have trouble keeping a job. Their enormous pain, low self-worth, and self-loathing are directed inward and lead to the self-harm and suicidal feelings that researchers and therapists believe, incorrectly, typify all people with BPD.

If you have BPD and meet these criteria—including you self-identify as having BPD—you are of the "conventional" type, and I did not write this book for you or about you. This book focuses on the "unconventional" high-conflict type who may have BPD, NPD, or traits of both.

The Unconventional Type

People with BPD in the "unconventional" group do not identify as having BPD or any other mental health condition. They take the pain, emptiness, low self-worth, and self-loathing typical of the conventional individual and project it outward, taking characteristics about themselves that they don't like and projecting them on the people who care about them most. It's like feeling overweight and calling someone else chubby. To cope with their unwanted feelings, they find a target of blame—mostly you. They will insist that all the problems you have with them are due to your many faults—things like you won't "improve" yourself, "make" them happy, or capitulate to all their demands. To control their environment and feel better about themselves, they rage, blame, criticize, and make false accusations. They may even become physically violent.

Unconventional individuals with BPD usually hide their disorder from people outside the family. They hold jobs, sometimes impressive ones, and are typically more independent than the conventional types. They mostly fiercely refuse to accept help. If they do go to counseling, it may be because someone has given them an ultimatum. Forced therapy, however, seldom works. They are stuck in denial as much as an alcoholic who gets sloppy drunk every day and has blackouts, yet insists they don't have a problem.

Types of NPD

There are two types of narcissism: the confident, charming, textbook "grandiose" type and the "covert" or "vulnerable" type. You can easily find examples of grandiose narcissism in politicians, celebrities, and CEOs. A vulnerable (or covert) NPD can appear modest and humble. They can fake empathy. But mostly, they want empathy and sympathy for the terrible things in the world that have made them professional victims. (People with BPD can also be professional victims.) Their emotional and verbal abuse is subtle, insidious, and passive-aggressive. They have the same traits as the grandiose NPD type, but they may attempt to hide those traits when they are around people they do not know well. Their demeaning actions are more subtle, and you may not notice that anything is wrong at first. But over time they drain you of energy. Signs that your loved one is a vulnerable NPD type include:

- They may be introverted and shy.

- They act as though they are the center of the universe. They are always thinking about themselves, not others—even in extreme situations.

- They are especially sensitive to criticism, even when criticism was not intended. For example, you might make a different decision than they would or listen to different music. They don't understand that you're a separate person who is entitled to have their own opinions.

- As I said, they have a victim mentality. For example, after a woman had been fired for cause five times, it didn't occur to look at her own behavior as a reason for the job losses.

Reflection

After reading this chapter, what stands out to you?

_____

_____

_____

_____

_____

_____

_____

_____

_____

What have you learned in this chapter that you want to put into action?

_____

_____

_____

_____

_____

_____

_____

_____

_____

CHAPTER 2

Borderline and Narcissistic Personality Disorders: The Similarities

In this chapter, I cover the similarities between people with BPD and people with NPD. I have compiled this list of similarities based on my twenty-five years of working with family members, partners, and loved ones of high-conflict people, as well as my research, both formal and informal. I originally created the following list for *Stop Walking on Eggshells for Partners*. There's a lot of information here, but I encourage you to stick with it because it will be useful when you are building skills to improve your relationship with your loved one and making tough decisions about kids, custody, and whether or not to remain in the partnership. You may find it useful to flip back to this chapter and review the similarities more than once.

Reality Is Based on Feelings

People with borderline personality disorder (BPD) or narcissistic personality disorder (NPD) often rely on their feelings to shape their reality, almost like children do. This concept is known as "emotional reasoning," where emotions are perceived as facts. They might ignore or dismiss actual evidence, similar to how someone avoids reading articles that challenge their strong beliefs. This confusion between feelings and facts usually stems from negative thoughts that are automatic and uncontrollable.

Splitting, or All-or-Nothing Thinking

Some people consider splitting to be a BPD trait only, but it also applies to people with NPD. Splitting means that a person can't integrate the good and bad aspects of people, situations, and themselves. It's got to be one or the other. When someone is bad, they're evil, and when they're good, they're angelic. Splitting can last hours, days, weeks, or years before the person with BPD or NPD switches (and they don't always switch).

Splitting is called a "primitive" defense mechanism because it's common in young children, for example when their feelings about their parents depend on whether they get a cookie before dinner or not. But people with BPD or NPD are stuck in this stage, and it makes them very difficult to deal with because when they feel one way, they can't remember ever feeling the opposite. People with NPD tend to "split people black" who threaten their self-image or who they perceive to have wronged them in some way, while people with BPD split when someone triggers one of their hot buttons, like abandonment.

Idealizing and Devaluing People

No one can meet the constant needs of someone with BPD or NPD and still have time for work, sleep, eating, or their own life. If you are in a relationship with an HCP, at the start of the relationship your partner may have thought you were perfect and could fix their deep emotional issues. But when they realized you're just a regular person and not someone who could magically heal them (BPD) or make them feel special all the time (NPD), they began to see you in a negative light. Things they liked about you before now annoy them. Don't be surprised by this change—it's normal. Idealization turns into devaluation, just like the seasons change. It's important to understand that the disorder is separate from the person. You can love the person and hate the disorder. However, they still need to work on changing their behavior if they want to maintain a relationship with you.

Having Feelings of Shame and Worthlessness

Why do I manipulate? It's to avoid feeling shame. Because of shame, I wear a mask. If it's on tightly, I feel prideful and safe. But if it starts to slip, I can't handle the shame, and I hide, lie to myself, or get angry at someone. Almost everything I do revolves around shame: what I do, what I don't do, and what I tell people about myself. People bring on shame by pointing out my flaws or mistakes, questioning my actions, ending the relationship, rebuffing me in public, talking about me, and even asking me questions that I don't want to answer—especially in front of others. Anything that might embarrass someone else causes me to cry rivers of shame.

Shame feels scary, like I am exposed to the world—and not just a naked kind of exposed. It's an eviscerated, everyone-can-see-your-innards kind of thing. If someone makes me feel ashamed, I go into a fight-or-flight response just because of the sheer terror of the situation. It's an unbelievably cruel and unnecessary thing to do to me, and if you cause me shame, you are an evil, hateful person, and I need to take you down.

—**Nick,** who has BPD and NPD

Guilt and shame are two different emotions. People feel guilt for something they've done, while shame centers on your very identity as a person. It's associated with self-disgust, self-contempt, self-loathing, and feelings of worthlessness. Toxic shame spins into other emotions, like anger, and makes a person feel small and worthless. People who have a loved one with these personality disorders often feel the same way when it comes to shame. They just deal with it differently. For example, they think of everyone's needs but their own because it makes them feel worthwhile.

Unstable Relationships Due to Difficulty with Emotional Intimacy

My wife with BPD wants intimacy but fears it at the same time. She has to be in control of it. When we are emotionally intimate, she says, "I am so scared that you are going to hurt me since I am so vulnerable now." I assure her that when she talks about her abusive background, it only makes me love her more. But she always finds some way to "prove" that I don't love her—for example, not answering the phone fast enough. She never completely trusts me, which hurts.

—Regan

A. J. Mahari (2009), a breakup and codependency recovery coach for more than thirty years who has recovered from BPD, pinpoints two fears—abandonment and engulfment—as one reason why emotional intimacy is difficult for people with BPD. She writes:

> Not only do people with BPD fear intimacy, but they are often not capable of it in an adult way. It's true that they crave to be close to someone, which is driven by very childlike emotional neediness that revolves around them trying to get their needs met through others, including trying to get some sense of "self" through another person.
>
> But being emotionally close to someone in an adult way requires being able to tolerate distance. [People with BPD] cannot tolerate the ebb and flow—the moving in and out—between closeness (intimacy) and distance. Intimacy often leaves the [person] stressed by the fear of engulfment, or being too crowded in. When that happens, they may generate emotional chaos and conflict to create some distance from their love object. This gives them temporary relief from engulfment fears.

People with NPD are also bad at intimacy. They can be good at emotional *intensity*, such as making a grand gesture on Valentine's Day. They can give you flowers and candy, but not a piece of themselves, which they keep buried because it is composed of shame and feelings of worthlessness. To build intimacy in a relationship, you need to be open and vulnerable and talk about what's deepest in your heart. But people with NPD use their disorder as a shield to keep others from getting too close. They must remain defended against outside threats, like their partner sharing their innermost self. Their conversations are transactional, and their goal in discussions is to win, look superior, and get the other person to do their bidding. None of this supports any kind of emotional intimacy.

Victim Mentality

My husband has either quit or been fired from six sales jobs in the last ten years. We have had to uproot our family six times. If you ask him, all his bosses were idiots or had it in for him. He takes no responsibility for this. He goes on and on about how his bosses are jealous of him, or have it out for him, and he is the poor victim. I know it's because he had a terrible childhood, but I'm sick of my children always being the new kids at school.

—Heather

Playing the victim makes people feel safe and comfortable, especially people with BPD, who hope that by playing the victim, their loved one will care for them. People with NPD may *feel* like a victim, but they also *play* the victim because it gives them a chance to gain attention.

People who struggle with a victim mentality are convinced that life is not only beyond their control but is deliberately out to get them. A victim mentality leads to blame, finger-pointing, and pity parties. Pessimism, fear, and anger also contribute to a victim mentality, as does extreme emotional sensitivity.

Stuck in Childhood

I always say I have three kids: my ten-year-old, my twelve-year-old, and my husband.

—**Dennis**

Developmentally speaking, people with BPD or NPD seem to get "stuck" or impaired at early levels of development. People with BPD get stuck at age eighteen months to twenty-four months, and people with NPD get stuck at about age six. This is their "emotional age." Part of them functions in an adult way: They can hold a high-level job, for example. But their ability to navigate complex relationships, see themselves clearly, and handle their emotional escalations have not developed past childhood.

You can see childish behaviors in BPD and NPD traits, such as blaming others for everything, lying, name-calling, poor impulse control, protests at separation, problems with sharing, lack of awareness of others' emotions, needing to be the center of attention, and all-or-nothing thinking (splitting). Developmental psychologists say there are optimal times when learning patterns of human interaction are much easier and after that time, it may be difficult or impossible to fully learn new ways of interacting (Fjelstad 2013).

Extreme Rages

The rage part is what scares me. It also creates great anxiety in my mind, as I am really worried about what I might do. I know that someone only needs to say the wrong thing (quite innocently on their part) and I will potentially turn into a wild animal. The anxiety and fear of losing my temper can build up to the point that I am literally shaking and cannot concentrate. The longer this goes on, the bigger the explosion of anger. I will try my very best to avoid any potential trigger situation, even to the point that I am almost paralyzed by indecision and fear of my own potential rage.

If it unfortunately does turn into a full-on fit of anger, well, that's when things get worrying. Property will be destroyed. My voice takes on a very deep and completely different tone. My lungs will project words so loudly that people nearby will stop to see what's going on. The recipient of the anger will have the most insulting and harsh personal insults literally spat out to them through bared teeth. Physical violence follows. And afterward, it is virtually impossible to rebuild any sort of relationship with the recipient.

—**George,** who has BPD and NPD

A rage attack can happen in an instant without warning, which causes loved ones to walk on eggshells. For some people, anger is a substitute emotion for feeling sad, hurt, guilt, disappointment, or shame. When a person is angry, they feel energized and powerful instead of vulnerable. Showing those other emotions can seem "weak," and most people don't want to explore those underlying feelings.

People with BPD rage for many of the same reasons. Rage isn't just an emotional reaction; it's key to their defense mechanism. People with BPD are unhappy when:

1. You aren't immediately available the moment they want to talk with you.

2. You pay attention to someone they fear could displace them.

3. Anyone gives them any kind of negative attention (such as criticism) or fails to give them positive attention (not saying "hi" when passing in the hallway, for example).

4. You want closeness when they want distance, or you want distance when they want closeness.

5. You go somewhere without them, especially for an extended length of time.

6. They feel rejected.

7. They feel misunderstood.

8. They feel ignored or invisible.

9. They are invalidated or perceive that their feelings are wrong, bad, invalid, or unimportant.

Lack of Accountability

Rule one: My partner is never at fault, to blame, or wrong. Rule two: See rule one.

—Betsy

While you must pay with blood for each of your transgressions, your loved one will never be accountable for any of their actions. Accepting accountability means admitting that they were wrong, and they are never wrong. Because of splitting, people with BPD or NPD think that one mistake makes them a mistake. So, lashing out is an important survival tactic. Without it, they would lose face and feel the shame creeping out of the vault.

Pathological Lying

Most of the time I don't even know when I'm lying because I'm lying to myself too. When I do know I am lying, I see it as a way to avoid shame, and I feel entitled to avoid my shame. In that case, it feels justifiable to lie, and it feels like I am rightfully trying to protect myself. I thought nothing of this for a long time. Now I know a little better.

—Aaron, who has BPD and NPD

People with BPD and NPD lie, especially those with NPD. On my website for loved ones of people with BPD and NPD, I found that 20 percent of the searches had to do with lying. Lying includes keeping secrets, omission (telling the incomplete truth), not speaking up when asked a direct question, making up facts that are not true, embellishing the truth in a misleading way, and insisting that the truth is false.

When you catch them red-handed, they will blame you for seeing through the lie, tell more lies, play the victim, make excuses, throw a fit about how unfair and selfish you are, or any combination of the above. Some people with BPD may lie spontaneously, while some people with NPD do it in a more manipulative way. But they both do it to cover up their feelings of shame and worthlessness and, for the person with NPD, to keep their special and entitled false self intact and avoid a narcissistic injury.

Extreme Jealousy

My wife goes crazy when I watch a certain TV program because she's convinced I have a crush on the main actress. She told me she didn't want me to watch it because of that. So I watch it when she's not at home.

—Ken

People with BPD can be extremely jealous to the point of ridiculousness. One man was "forbidden" by his wife with BPD to answer the phone at work—his own business—because there might be a woman on the other end. The thought of you with another lover strikes at the heart of their fear of abandonment and rejection. Someone with NPD feels possessive about their sources of narcissistic supply and will be sensitive to anything that threatens it.

Infidelity in Romantic Relationships

After I broke up with my narcissistic boyfriend, he was involved with another woman within a week. I think he was seeing her before we broke up. It makes me feel better when I imagine him doing the same thing to her as he did to me.

—Doreen

While they question you about any disloyalty, one of their survival strategies is to keep a potential partner in mind or waiting in the wings in the event you aren't meeting their overwhelming needs. One of the most active topics in online forums where partners hang out is about cheating. The authors of one study say, "Relative to non-narcissists, narcissistic individuals tend to be less committed to their romantic partners and to play games with their romantic partners; they also tend to be less satisfied with their relationships and engage in infidelity more often" (Altınok and Kılıç 2020).

Since people with both disorders need others to give them what they cannot provide for themselves, cheating or having someone shiny and new waiting for them gives them the feeling of control.

You Can't Make Them Happy

My husband knows I'm a decent person who doesn't lie, cheat, or steal. He complains he isn't happy with me and starts fights knowing I will never admit to things I didn't do or agree with his interpretation of why I did something. He will just say I'm lying about why I (supposedly) did something, and it's always for deceitful or hateful reasons. He gets himself all upset for nothing, and he won't believe me.

Your loved one has a few thousand complaints about you. They are sure that if you just change, they will be happy. I hear that from loved ones, partners, and family members all the time who believe that if they can just change in some way, their loved one will be pleased with them and the complaints will stop.

All of this is untrue. You could turn yourself inside out and they would still be unhappy. Your loved one is morose because of the disorder, and you happen to be the handiest target to blame. They feel upset and aren't self-aware enough to understand it's coming from them, so they convince themself the problems emanate from you. Someone with NPD can put you down because they need to feel better than someone. They believe that if you're of inferior status, their status is raised. People with BPD feel such intense pain that they try to spread it around, in hopes they won't feel so bad. Remember, they're never accountable and they can't admit fault.

This is a good news-bad news kind of explanation. On the good side, I'll say it again: *Their unhappiness is not your fault.* The bad news is that you can't change something about yourself to increase their happiness. You don't have that power, and you never did. What is happening is inside their mind. Becoming happy is an inside job, and true happiness lies in getting treatment for the disorder.

Using Survival Strategies to Maintain Control

In chapter 1, I explained that people with BPD need other people to manage their moods, while those with NPD use other people to manage their self-esteem. Not being able to depend on themselves represents a huge loss of control. Additionally, when other people provide them what they need, it doesn't last long. They need another "hit" very soon. Therefore, they try to exert control through a wide variety of survival strategies that may make them feel better—for a little bit.

These strategies have two things in common: First, they are meant to control their environment—especially the people in it—so they don't have to experience their many fears, such as being thought of as unimportant or inferior, or to feel ignored or humiliated. Having control also wards off feelings of shame and worthlessness. Second, the strategies are intended to make you feel small, so they have power and control over you. Some of these strategies are unconscious; others aren't. It really doesn't matter. What matters is their effect on you.

These techniques, or survival strategies, keep you confused, intimidated, off guard, and feeling stuck. The high-conflict person makes it seem like they're in the driver's seat when it comes to defining reality. Naturally, they will tell you they are forced to do these things because it's your fault. It isn't. These are survival skills, and your loved one is the last person whose critiques you should take personally. For some, to make themselves feel good, they need others to feel bad.

Here is a list of control-based survival strategies:

- Acting jealous and possessive. In a romantic relationship, this can look like insisting you are interested in other people

- Having unrealistic expectations, such as expecting you to do all the housework and childcare or expecting you to fulfill their every need this very minute

- Seeing everything as a personal attack, which prevents you from bringing up anything you want them to work on

- Using physical force, including kicking, pushing, shoving, hitting, or otherwise making physical contact toward you in an unwanted way

- Trying to isolate you from family and friends

- Giving you the silent treatment

- In romantic relationships, forcing sexual activity, which includes touching you in unwelcome sexual ways when you're asleep, expecting you to have sex whenever they demand it, or persuading you to have sex to avoid a big argument

- Gaslighting, making you doubt your reality, like saying, "I didn't yell very loudly. You were the one who screamed at me"

- Using emotional blackmail, fear, obligation, or guilt to get their way

- Promising that things will change (but they never do)

- Making threats, like they will divorce you or not let you see the kids, including vague threats like, "You'll be sorry if you do that!"

- DARVOing (Deny, Argue, Reverse Victim and Offender) when confronted with misdeeds or the fact that they have a problem

- Using sarcasm like a blade

- Throwing or destroying property, especially your prized possessions

- Deliberately misremembering

- Belittling you or calling you names

- Withholding affection or purposely not meeting your needs

- Devaluing and dismissing your viewpoint

- Putting down your interests and opinions

- Constantly monitoring you and trying to get you to believe you need their permission to spend time with someone, spend time alone, or have your own interests

Blaming and Criticizing

It was somehow my fault that the blanket was too warm.

—Kevin

While most people would try to cope with shame and worthlessness through therapy or in some other way, those with BPD or NPD have a different strategy. They deny they have these feelings and "project" them (plus any number of negative traits they secretly identify with) onto people close to them whom they manipulate into feeling those feelings for them. Projection is taking an unwanted trait or feeling and attributing it to someone else. (As I said in the last chapter, it's like feeling overweight and calling someone else chubby.) Sometimes the projection has a bit of truth in it (you could stand to lose a few pounds), but your loved one will twist it into a Greek tragedy. Projecting their shame onto you is one of the main survival mechanisms of most high-conflict people.

The first step to feeling better is understanding that because of their internal programming, your loved one is attributing their own painful traits and feelings to you. No matter what their specific criticisms are, it's never really been about you at all. Their words and actions are really about their fears, their feelings about themself, and their need for control.

Needing to Exert Power and Control

Essentially, high-conflict people need power and control. They do this with very little empathy (BPD) or no empathy (NPD) because their survival strategies are needed for, well, survival. Only the fittest survive. Some of this is done unconsciously; some know what they are doing.

For example, people with BPD will test your love for them because of fear of abandonment. They will push you past your limits or act unreasonably. The logic goes like this: If you really love them, you should be willing to put aside all your own desires and concentrate on fulfilling their needs. For example, if you and your loved one agree to meet at a certain time and place, they may show up an hour late. If you "fail" the test by becoming irritated or giving up and going home, they may feel their unworthiness has been confirmed. This makes the world more predictable and therefore safer. If you "pass" the test by tolerating their actions, they may escalate the behavior (perhaps by showing up many hours late next time), until you finally blow up in anger. Then you become the bad guy, and they become the victim. You may be wondering, *What kind of test is this? No matter what happens, we both fail!* You're right. It doesn't make any sense in your world. But it does in the borderline world (Mason and Kreger 2020). Other examples of exerting power and control for someone with BPD include (Greenburg 2021):

- "If you love me, you will announce our engagement on social media (even though we have only been dating for a month)"

- Crying and threatening to harm themself if you don't do something they ask immediately

- Making you get out of the car during a fight or insisting you let them off on the highway

While people with BPD are trying to avoid abandonment (for example, by isolating you from other people), power and control strategies for the person with NPD are done for several reasons. They can only see their ideas and preferences as meaningful, so they want to control you to:

- Get their way

- Establish dominance in the relationship

- Prove they are above you in the status hierarchy

- Control access to resources

Here are a few ways they might do this:

- Asking you to move to another state where you have no friends, family, or job for support

- Offering to take over a "chore" (such as paying bills or investing money) and then not giving you the information you need

- Over time, taking over more and more of your life decisions

- Calling you selfish and ungrateful if you complain or want to do something for yourself

- Trying to make you feel too stupid and inadequate to do a particular task or take on a responsibility, for example, "I am better with numbers and computers than you. I can get it done faster and more efficiently."

- Accusing you of being paranoid if you call them controlling

- Alienating you from your friends and family by demonizing them and making excuses why the two of you should not ever see them

- Keeping you up all night fighting until you give in

As I explained in the last chapter, people with BPD can act very differently from each other. For example, some want treatment very much (the conventional type), and others can't imagine it because nothing is their fault (the unconventional type). People of the conventional type turn their pain inward and are suicidal and self-harm, while those of the unconventional type project unwanted attributes onto other people. Some people with NPD (mostly those of the vulnerable type) do not cause the conflict that those of the grandiose type do.

Unfortunately, it's unlikely that your loved one will ever see a therapist for a possible diagnosis. I assure you, unless a therapist actively has a practice for people with BPD or NPD, if you are well read on the topic, you are likely to know more than them about HCPs.

Reflection

After reading this chapter, what stands out to you?

_____

_____

_____

_____

_____

_____

_____

_____

_____

What have you learned in this chapter that you want to put into action?

_____

_____

_____

_____

_____

_____

_____

_____

_____

CHAPTER 3

Getting Together: Relationship Behavior Patterns

My therapist told me that my wife gave borderline personality disorder a bad name. When I asked her if she was crazy, the therapist said, "No, but she will make everyone around her crazy."

—A member of the Moving Forward online support group

Just like there are many ways of explaining behavior, there are many ways of describing the dynamics between high-conflict people and their loved ones. These change greatly depending on whether you're talking about parents and their children, siblings, friends, or other types of relationships. Each relationship is unique. But most people will find these repetitious themes.

Verbal and Emotional Abuse: "I'm Saying This to Make You a Better Person"

Although most HCPs do not intend to be verbally or emotionally abusive, their feelings cause them to act in ways that can feel like abuse to those around them.

What follows are some forms of emotional abuse outlined by author Beverly Engel (1990). If they apply to you, write an example or two that come to mind about how the activity takes place in your life. This will help you understand the material and retain it.

Domination. The person resorts to threats to get their own way.

_____

_____

_____

_____

_____

_____

_____

_____

Verbal assaults. This includes reprimanding, humiliating, criticizing, name-calling, screaming, threatening, excessive blaming, and using sarcasm in a cutting way. It also involves exaggerating other people's faults and making fun of them in front of others. Over time, this type of abuse erodes self-confidence and self-worth.

_____

_____

_____

_____

_____

_____

Abusive expectations. The other person makes unreasonable demands and expects that you will be their first priority—no matter what. This includes renouncing your own needs for attention and support.

_____

_____

_____

_____

_____

_____

_____

Unpredictable responses. This includes drastic mood changes or sudden emotional outbursts. Living with someone like this is extremely anxiety provoking. You may feel frightened, unsettled, and off-balance. This hypervigilance (constantly feeling "jumpy" and on guard against potential attacks) can even lead to physical illness and complex post-traumatic stress disorder.

_____

_____

_____

_____

_____

_____

Gaslighting. This involves denying a person's perceptions of events and conversations, especially those they know to be true. Depending upon the length of your relationship with your loved one, you may give them the benefit of the doubt and believe they live in this universe, not their alternate reality. It's essential that you believe your inner voice telling you that you are not selfish, that you didn't abuse them, and so forth.

_____

_____

_____

_____

_____

_____

Constant chaos. Deliberately starting arguments, creating drama, and being in constant conflict with others.

_____

_____

_____

_____

_____

_____

_____

_____

_____

Reflection

After reading this chapter, what stands out to you?

_____

_____

_____

_____

_____

_____

_____

_____

_____

What have you learned in this chapter that you want to put into action?

_____

_____

_____

_____

_____

_____

_____

_____

_____

_____

CHAPTER 4

Brainwashing 101: How High-Conflict Behavior Affects You

Unless you have a mind of steel, abuse doesn't slip off. It penetrates and erodes, chips away, and it does it slowly and invisibly, and all the while you're thinking you're doing a great job dealing with it. And one day you wake up and realize you've been decimated. And the healing is slow, painful work.

—A member of the Moving Forward online support community

Having a relationship with an HCP can affect people in very different ways, depending upon these primary factors:

- The type of relationship, e.g., parent/child vs. sibling/sibling. People who were raised by someone with BPD or NPD are profoundly affected, while people who have been friends for only a year are not as deeply affected.

- The specific actions of the HCP detailed in earlier chapters, i.e., acting out, the specific traits they display, and concurrent issues they might have (such as substance abuse).

- Your characteristics and personality traits. For example, you may have been raised in an environment in which you were expected to "rescue" your parent or sibling, and later in life, you may take on the same role with your HCP.

Another basic factor is whether you are in this relationship by choice.

Chosen relationships. This category is mostly made up of partners and friends. In this case, you may be able to compare your pre-HCP self to your post-HCP self, allowing you to assess how the relationship has changed your life for better and for worse.

Unchosen relationships. If the HCP in your life is your child, in-law, or anything but a parent or a sibling, you probably have a good idea of how your loved one has influenced you because you have years of your life as a basis for comparison. However, if your family member is your parent or a sibling, it can be hard to judge what your life would have been like without this person. But hopefully, you now have a better grasp of how this relationship has affected you.

Action Step: How the HCP in Your Life Affects You

What follows are some people's most common aspects of life that are affected by living with a person exhibiting HCP behavior. This exercise will help you pinpoint how the relationship is affecting you.

If you are in a chosen relationship (e.g., friend, partner) you may have forgotten what you were like before the relationship, depending upon how long it has lasted. Before doing this exercise, you may find it helpful to have a frank talk with friends and family. If your family member is unchosen (blood or family relation), it can be difficult to know what life would be like if your loved one wasn't an HCP. If so, your friends may be able to help you pinpoint what is "normal" and what is not. Either way, when doing the exercise, please be as honest as you can—which may mean going with your first, gut reaction.

Put a number in the space before each response to indicate the degree to which you feel affected. Use a scale of 0 to 4, where "0" means you're not affected at all, a "1" means you're mildly affected, a "2" means you're moderately affected, a "3" means you're strongly affected, and a "4" means you're severely affected. In the space after each response, note how you have been affected: positively, negatively, or whatever else is appropriate. Because of the many different kinds of relationships, not all these statements may apply to you. Just ignore those that don't fit in. If something important to you is not listed, write it in at the end.

My loved one has affected me in the following ways:

☐ My ability to trust _____

_____

☐ My ability to love _____

_____

☐ My sense of security _____

_____

☐ My vulnerability _____

_____

☐ My overall outlook on life _____

_____

☐ My ability to be intimate _____

_____

☐ My sexuality _____

_____

☐ My religious or spiritual beliefs _____

_____

☐ My ability to empathize _____

_____

☐ My finances _____

_____

☐ My cynicism toward life _____

_____

☐ My sense of purpose _____

_____

☐ My ability to get my needs met _____

_____

☐ The way I rear my child(ren) _____

_____

☐ My ability to set personal limits _____

_____

☐ My ability to be assertive _____

_____

☐ My method of dealing with problems _____

_____

☐ My legal worries _____

_____

☐ My self-esteem _____

_____

☐ My values _____

_____

☐ My physical health _____

_____

☐ My lifestyle _____

_____

☐ My career _____

_____

☐ My family relationships _____

_____

☐ My friendships _____

_____

☐ My feelings of competency _____

_____

Other important areas _____

_____

_____

_____

_____

_____

Action Step: What Are Your Needs and Wishes?

This Action Step is about *your* needs and wishes, especially those that have gone unmet. This is an important Action Step you will use later on in the book, so please give yourself plenty of time to go through it in detail. Read through all the instructions before you begin.

Step 1. Buy a pack of index cards—any color or size will do.

Step 2. Now, pretend that your HCP relationship doesn't exist and some spiritual being has given you the opportunity to design your own parent, partner, sibling, or whatever role they play in relation to you. On each index card, write down the ideal qualities you would like in a person who is going to fulfill that role. If the role is "partner," for example, you might write down "capacity for emotional intimacy." If it's a child, you might choose "a happy disposition." Remember, you're not writing down what you *have*, but what you *want* or *need*.

You can use your present situation for ideas, but don't stop there. Brainstorm, borrowing ideas from TV shows, books, music, movies, friends, or whatever else inspires you.

Write down items as they occur to you for a week or two—even over a month. As time goes by, you will probably come up with things that you've lost sight of, given up for dead, or tried to erase from your mind. If writing brings on strong emotions of anger, grief, or anything else, put a star by it and jot down your feelings. Do not censor yourself or deny needs that the logical parts of your brain think are unrealistic. In fact, tell your logical self to take a siesta and let your emotional self do the work. There is no "right" or "wrong" in this particular exercise.

Step 3. When you're done, you'll need some private space, some uninterrupted time, and a large flat surface, such as the floor or an empty dining room table. Spread your cards out, looking for themes such as common interests, emotional capacities, intellectual capabilities, personality traits, etc. Put each theme in a pile and give it a name.

Don't worry too much about the categories at this point. The goal is to get your thoughts organized around concepts that may have been little more than vague feelings until now.

Step 4. Once you have categorized your overall needs using the cards, divide the cards into two stacks, representing your higher and lower priorities.

Step 5. Then take the higher-priority pile and divide it into these categories:

a. Needs that are fulfilled now

b. Needs your loved one might be able to fulfill if they chose to obtain treatment

c. Those they could not fulfill even if they wanted to

Step 6: Write down each high-priority item in your notebook, along with a, b, or c, above. Keep all the cards; you will use them again later. As time goes by, add to them if you like.

This Action Step was designed to assist you in becoming more aware of your own needs and to help you begin the process of defining them for yourself. When we can't get something important out of a relationship and the lack of this causes pain, we often try to convince ourselves that we can do without it, that no one is perfect, and that the good things about the person make up for what we can't have.

These rationalizations may all be true. But no matter how deep we bury our longings, they don't go away. In fact, they shouldn't go away because our deepest longings often hold the keys to our most deeply held values and the forgotten parts of ourselves. Our rational self understands that you can't always get what you want. But our emotions don't give up that easily. While our rational brains are busy thinking about what we need to pick up at the store or some other mundane thing, our emotions are primed and ready to be triggered.

One Woman's Triggers

Claire wished that her husband Bob would be more spontaneously affectionate and desirous of her sexually. She tried to explain this to him as gently as she could, but Bob wasn't the spontaneous and desirous type. Despite Claire's efforts to communicate in a positive manner, the message he got from the discussion was, "Claire is criticizing me in a sensitive area and that makes me want to stay away from her." The more Claire tried to explain, the worse it got. So eventually, she decided to let it go. She felt secure in Bob's love. So she concentrated on what really counted: his loving actions. For instance, he always took her car in to get the oil changed. It wasn't what most people would call "romantic." But she hated tasks involving the car, and he knew it.

Several months later, Claire and Bob decided to have Bob's parents over for dinner. It was a social obligation Bob disliked. For various reasons, he and his parents were not close. But Claire made it as easy for him as she could, cooking up a storm, making friendly conversation, and smoothing over awkward moments.

Bob felt so appreciative of Claire's efforts that before dinner, as he watched her stirring something on the stove, her back to him, he gently lifted up her hair and kissed her slowly and sensually on the neck. Claire felt his warm lips and the stubble on his chin brush her neck. Suddenly she began to cry. In a split second, she realized how much she missed these little displays of affection and how much they meant to her. She cried because she didn't know if it would ever happen again. Bob's action triggered an emotional reaction to Claire's unmet intimacy needs.

Action Step: Giving Up Myths about High-Conflict People and Your Relationship

In order to change the way you view your loved one's behavior, you may have to give up some distorted thinking of your own. What follows is a list of some of the most popular myths about BPD and NPD, followed by descriptions of circumstances that are more likely to be true. These differ, of course, according to the person and type of relationship. Put a checkmark next to the myths that you need to give up. Circle those that you need to work on the most.

☐ "If something is wrong, it's my fault." HCPs are exceptionally good at convincing people of their flaws because they really, truly believe what they're saying (feelings equal facts). If you felt good about yourself before, your loved one can change this. If you had a problem with self-esteem in the first place, you are especially at risk. Before you accept responsibility for anything or allow yourself to be labeled, make sure that what they say is confirmed by others whom you trust to give you truthful, non-disordered feedback.

☐ "Love conquers everything." The Beatles notwithstanding, you do need more than love to solve biological problems or issues that were there long before you were on the scene. Recent brain research shows that there are differences in the actual brain structures of people with BPD and NPD when compared with people who don't have the disorders. Specifically, there are differences in the size of the part of the brain involved in synthesizing memories, called the hippocampus (Driessen et al. 2000). Love can do many wonderful things, but it can actually worsen the situation if it prevents you from setting firm personal limits and observing them.

☐ "My loved one's behavior reflects on me and is my responsibility." You cannot control their behavior. If you know from experience that you will be put in an embarrassing situation, don't put yourself there. Take separate cars, refuse an invitation, or do things alone or with friends. This is difficult for parents because they are responsible for their child's behavior, and a lot of it takes place in the home. However, you can modify your child's behavior if you know how. To find out, obtain the book *Stop Walking on Eggshells for Parents*. People in relationships may want to check out *Stop Walking on Eggshells for Partners*.

☐ "Setting limits is impossible." Setting limits is entirely possible. The secret is deciding beforehand what your limits are, what to do whenever they are not observed, and to be consistent with your response.

Let's take it to some extremes, just to make the point. What would you do if your loved one held a gun to your head? Or, if they are your partner, what would you do if you found them having an affair with your best friend in your own bedroom? If they are your child, what would you do if they stabbed one of their siblings?

Most HCPs know how far they can push before you say "enough." The problem is that line is too close to your "breaking point"—the line that, if crossed, will lead to drastic consequences. What you need to do is clarify what behavior you will and won't accept, and observe your boundaries.

☐ "I need/must have their love and approval." This is a common myth, especially among people who have an HCP parent. We would all like to have love and approval from the important people in our lives. But when we have to give up part of ourselves to get it, we lose something more important: our own integrity. You can obtain love from many places—love that doesn't hurt or require that you give up your boundaries.

Getting "approval" isn't really necessary unless your loved one is your supervisor at work. *What is holding you back is not the lack of approval but your feeling that you need it.* Remember that HCPs are doing the best they can with the tools that they have. If your expectations are high, you may be disappointed. If your expectations are low, you may increase your chances of being pleasantly surprised.

☐ "My loved one is responsible for my happiness or unhappiness." You can spend a few decades, if you want to, trying to get what you need or what you would like to see change about your high conflict loved one. People who do that have not really accepted their loved one has a disorder that radically changes their thoughts, feelings, and behavior. They did not choose to have this condition. But they do.

Accepting that your loved one is an HCP doesn't mean accepting the way they treat others. It only means accepting reality. It gives you a place to start. OK, my loved one is mentally ill. What should I do to protect my family? This workbook will have some tools. My other books also spend a lot of time with these tools. My book *The Essential Family Guide to Borderline Personality Disorder* goes over five tools that should be used in a certain order.

☐ "Logical statements or arguments are useful tools." It takes time for some people with an HCP loved one to learn that logic simply does not work. That's because their emotions are in control, and emotions are much more powerful than logic. Coming to grips with this fact may require you to give up some degree of control and focus instead on your own feelings.

☐ "Try, try again, and then try the same thing again." A very similar quagmire. Everyone is different, and your loved one will react differently at different times. If something doesn't work, give it up.

Here's a small story about someone who did just that. It involves a borderline mother and a grown son who live far apart. Because it only happened once a year when he visited her, the son noticed a pattern. The day before he would board a plane to head back home, his mother would try to provoke him into a major argument. He guessed that she was feeling abandoned. She wasn't going to stop, so he had to have a strategy for how he was going to protect himself from the rages. The arguments had caused him much misery over the years until finally he decided to respond differently. Fighting her was exhausting and useless.

The next time he visited, he was ready for the day-before-leaving assault. As it had previously, the attack came out of nowhere, was cruel and hurtful, and was completely pointless. At a restaurant, his mother accused him of not caring or knowing about her life. Rather than argue, he just mildly recited everything he had learned about her during that visit.

When that tactic didn't draw him into an argument, his mother accused him of being self-centered. He calmly replied that she probably had a point, since he had just lost his job and was focused on that. The mother, probably frustrated that her usual techniques weren't working, disowned the son, saying they had "nothing in common" and she "never wanted to speak to him again." He calmly took a bite of his hamburger, swallowed, and said that although they might have nothing in common, they could still get through one meal together. He suggested that his mother might feel differently in the future and invited her to call him if she wanted to—or not to if she didn't. He smiled and drank his soda while his mother glared at him. He wasn't following the script. The son knew that his mother did indeed need him; she had called him frequently ever since her second husband had died. In fact, she was quite alone, and he knew that she needed him more than he needed her.

His mother finally gave up and ate the rest of her dinner in silence. The son resumed talking as if nothing had happened. And sure enough, three weeks after he returned home, his mother began calling again as if the argument had never taken place. Several months later, she denied that the incident had ever happened.

He learned some valuable lessons from the restaurant scene: First, he wouldn't be pushed around. Second, he didn't need to bite the bait dangling from his mother's fish-hook. In fact, he felt sorry for her—sorry that she was getting older, had no partner, and was alone in a faraway city. But the most important lesson was that he could become "manipulation proof" and could appreciate her genuine feelings of love and caring.

☐ "Other people are being emotionally abused, not me." Emotional and verbal abuse are an HCP's stock-in-trade. In my experience working with people who have an HCP loved one, I have found that men especially don't want to admit that they're being emotionally abused because they think it makes them less of a man. They believe it's their responsibility to fix their partner, which is impossible without treatment. Male partners like to think of themselves as "nice guys" who give in to their partner's wishes, have no self-care, and are afraid to assert themselves. It's something they need to change when it comes to their loved one.

☐ "You can't hold them accountable for their behavior." This goes something like this: Since BPD is a biological disorder, then no one should be angry at their loved one any more than if they had cancer or some other physical illness. The problem with this comparison is that someone with BPD or NPD who won't accept treatment is like a diabetic who won't stay on a diet or take their insulin. Avoiding treatment accomplishes nothing but making their own life and that of other people unnecessarily miserable. Your loved one didn't choose to have a disorder, but they can choose whether or not to obtain treatment.

☐ "I will be a victim until my loved one changes." If you get nothing else out of this book, know that if you change your responses to their behavior, you will alter the dynamic between you.

Going through the Grieving Process

At one point in time, you had an ideal relationship in mind for you and your loved one. They were going to be a great parent, partner, or child. Your child was supposed to graduate with honors and then go to college. You looked forward to having a great relationship with your grown child. You and your partner were going to have a great sex life. You have expectations that were not met and you've been hurt—even betrayed—in unexpected ways.

Depending upon the length and the type of relationship you are in, you will need to grieve what you never had, what you had and lost, and what you want that you can't seem to get. The first step is to identify your feelings—especially the ones you've learned to deny or repress.

Action Step: Grief Awareness

Pick an unpleasant event in your life that doesn't involve your loved one. If you are bold enough and feel strong enough to go for the gold, pick an event that you could describe as the worst thing that ever happened to you. If you aren't feeling quite so strong and bold as that, you might want to try something a bit milder, such as your most embarrassing moment. Take a few moments, relax, and recall that scenario. Picture it in your mind in detail.

What were the sights? Sounds? Smells? Was there any particular feeling that seemed to be lingering in the air, such as an air of tension, or a sense of comfort and relaxation? Recall each one of these details as vividly as you can. Give yourself four or five minutes to absorb that situation again.

Once you have that memory vividly in your mind, start paying attention to your body and how you're physically reacting to the memory. How do your hands feel? Tense? Warm? Cold? Clammy? Notice the feelings in other parts of your body: How does your head feel? Your face? Your feet? Your stomach? Your neck? Your arms and chest?

When you have taken enough time to notice these feelings in some detail, think back once more. But this time, think back to a recent unpleasant experience with your loved one. Are the feelings similar? What is similar about them, and what is different? This will give you some clues as to whether your loved one is creating new painful feelings or whether they are actually reawakening old feelings based on painful memories you had tried to put aside.

What was it like to complete that exercise? What came up for you?

_____

_____

_____

_____

_____

_____

_____

_____

_____

One of the things that keeps people in unhealthy relationships is the fact that they may have unresolved grief from previous events in their lives. Developing the ability to deal with present relationships means finishing old grief from previous situations.

For some of us, that grief may be related to painful childhood circumstances in which we learned to "tough it out" as best we could. Even though we might have steeled ourselves to those circumstances, it does not necessarily mean that we didn't still feel some pain or sadness underneath. Recovering from unhealthy relationships and dealing with them in healthier ways generally requires us to reawaken some old painful wounds, even though it seems like it would be so much more pleasant and easier just to leave them alone. But if we want to strengthen ourselves to withstand the demands of unhealthy relationships, we simply do not have that luxury.

The first section of this workbook has been your "basic training." You've looked at your situation and determined where you are and perhaps how you got there. In this next section, we'll look at how you can make changes that will help you control your own life while maintaining some kind of connection with the HCP in your life, if that's what you choose.

Reflection

After reading this chapter, what stands out to you?

_____

_____

_____

_____

_____

_____

_____

_____

What have you learned in this chapter that you want to put into action?

_____

_____

_____

_____

_____

_____

_____

_____

CHAPTER 5

Beyond Denial: Accepting What You Cannot Change (and Changing What You Can)

I thought that if I worked harder, more often, kept the house a bit cleaner, surely he would love me. But he didn't. Giving up hope saved my life.

—Charles

Change is difficult, but it is possible. One important thing you need to know, though, is that change is even harder for HCPs than it is for you. As with alcoholism, a common symptom of being an HCP is denial. An alcoholic will drink until they black out every night and proclaim they are "fine"; a person who shows all the traits of BPD or NPD may deny the disorder's existence in themself, but curiously find it in many other people in their life.

But your loved one isn't the only one in denial. While some family members, partners, and friends are relieved to discover that this condition has a diagnosis, some think of the disorder as a temporary setback that will disappear with time, with more love or the right kind of loving, or by some other means that doesn't involve time, hard work in therapy, and perhaps medication.

Relationship Outcomes with BPD

If someone you love has BPD, you may find that one of the following will happen after you understand the role the disorder plays in their behavior. Now you have choices to make.

- You deny that BPD is a problem and do nothing. The status quo reigns.

- Your loved one denies that BPD is a problem. The status quo reigns, except that you go nuts trying to change them.

- You accept the person as they are and allow the disorder to claim the happiness in your life.

- You radically accept that your loved one has BPD, but protect yourself with the techniques in this workbook. You may work with a therapist.

- Your loved one acknowledges there is a problem, but does very little to accomplish lasting change. They may select an inexperienced therapist who will not dig very deep, who is unfamiliar with the disorder, or who can be easily conned.

- Your loved one will acknowledge they have a problem and will work hard with a good psychiatric team to overcome the disorder—a process that may take years.

Of course, everyone wants an immediate awakening, a miracle cure such as a pill or therapy that will work overnight and turn everything all around. I haven't personally seen such a miracle, but I have seen people witness their children being emotionally abused while the other parent waits for this miracle to happen.

Being human, you want your loved one to understand you, validate your experiences, apologize, empathize, and stop borderline behaviors that threaten the relationship. People with BPD may or may not ask, but most of them want their friends and family members to understand their pain, fulfill their needs, and assuage their feelings of emptiness, worthlessness, pain, and other painful feelings.

No matter how much you love someone, you cannot make them love themself and make the best choices for themself. This is one of the hardest things to accept. The person with the disorder must, with help from a clinician, support groups, and other resources, conquer their own demons.

Action Step: Past Efforts to Change Your High-Conflict Loved One

Let's take a look at your efforts to change your loved one and see how they've worked out.

Below, you'll find three blank columns with different headings. On the left, make a list of everything you asked your loved one to change about themself, from small to large. Next to this list, write down all the things you did to motivate your loved one to change, in each case. Include things like nagging, giving rewards, punishments, and ultimatums—whatever you tried. Then, on the right, write down the results of your efforts. Did these behaviors change? If so, for how long? Were there any unexpected results? Think carefully about whether you changed your loved one or harmed yourself.

Change Wanted	Methods Tried	Results

As I said before, you may feel responsible for "fixing" or "rescuing" your loved one from their own self-defeating habits and ways of thinking. The benefit of this belief is that it gives you a sense of control. But it's an illusion. You can't fundamentally change anyone. You can show them a path and talk about the benefits of that path, you can manipulate them for a short time through rewards and punishments. But as soon as you stop the reward or punishment, their old, familiar ways of thinking and behaving will return. This next Action Step will help you feel that.

Action Step: A Change Experiment

Pick a habit you want to change, something that is a goal of yours that gives you a direct benefit, such as you would like to take a walk every day, eat breakfast, or spend more quality time with your kids. Make the goal reasonable and within reach. If you succeed, what will the benefits be? Write these benefits down and refer to them throughout the week.

_____

_____

_____

_____

_____

Spend a month or so working hard on your goal and then answer these questions:

1. What habit did you choose to change?

_____

_____

_____

_____

_____

2. Did you change your habit? If not, how long were you able to keep it up?

_____

_____

_____

_____

_____

3. Was it hard to remember to make this change?

_____

_____

_____

_____

_____

4. Did it feel less strange as the time progressed?

_____

_____

_____

_____

_____

5. Did the fact that this was something you wanted and you chose affect your attitude, success, or willingness to try this experiment?

_____

_____

_____

_____

_____

This Action Step should have reinforced that change is difficult, even if you want to change. If your loved one is not willing to change their behavior, what is the chance they will get better? Success depends upon keeping the benefits of the change at the top of your mind.

If changing something about yourself that you want to change is difficult, imagine how difficult it is for people with a personality disorder to change—even if they want to. And if they don't want to—if the coping mechanism seems to be working for them—there is almost no chance they will change, unless they're manipulated into it by an ultimatum. Ultimatums and other manipulative devices rarely create lasting change, however. A person needs encouragement, intrinsic or extrinsic rewards, necessary skills, and something to replace the thing that is lost. This is one reason why professional help is so necessary for HCPs. Losing a coping mechanism without something to put in its place is very frightening.

Identity Issues

Change is especially difficult if it changes our self-definition. Eva, for example, has had a difficult life. Her parents divorced when she was an infant, she was molested when she was ten, she has lived in poverty, and members of her extended family have been killed. As much as Eva would like to change some of the dysfunctional ways she copes, she wonders who she would be without the pain she has been carrying around most of her life. That pain has defined her. It has made her who she is. Once you take that away, what is left? Such feelings need to be discussed with a mental health professional. With help, Eva can hopefully become the person she was meant to be while giving up mourning for the things she never had and the things she had and lost.

High-Conflict Behavior Is Not About You

Your loved one's capacity or desire to change is not in your control. You have to accept the fact that seeking treatment is entirely their decision. You can tell them how their actions and words make you feel and suggest solutions. But what they do with that information is out of your hands.

What *is* in your hands are your emotional reactions to their behavior. There is a saying posted in many workplaces: "A crisis on your part does not necessarily mean a crisis on my part."

If your loved one is having a crisis because you set a boundary, you don't have to respond to their complaints, protests, rages, or limit-testing. You can simply reiterate your limit and act confidently. For example, when a sick person with NPD wanted me to care for him, I refused to be yelled at and quietly said I would leave if the behavior continued. It stopped right away.

Detaching with Love

"Detach with love" should be your motto. You need to keep your life from being a series of HCP-related crises. The message to your loved one is: "I care about you, and I recognize that you must make your own choices in life. I can love you, but I can't live your life for you. I can point you in the right direction, but I can't push you down the path."

Your loved one is responsible for the crises they create. HCPs create dramas, consciously or unconsciously. You can make those emotional dramas your problem, or you can let your loved one handle them as best they can (given the appropriateness of the situation and their age).

If you take responsibility for their chaos, you risk reinforcing that behavior and causing yourself a lot of grief. If you let your loved one handle their own problems, it's more likely that they will learn how to take care of things themself or avoid dramas altogether.

Letting Go of Your Loved One's Problems

The first step in detaching with love is to let go of problems that do not really involve you. Naturally, your loved one will try to make you responsible either directly ("This is your fault!") or indirectly.

You can learn to emotionally let go of what you *can't* control. When your loved one tries to gaslight you, recognize it as gaslighting and move on.

What you can do is show love and concern while assuring your loved one they can handle the situation by themself. If you keep doing this consistently, your loved one will realize that they don't have to create tests to prove you love them. When you stop covering up mistakes, cleaning up messes, and taking responsibility for their problems, they can begin to grow emotionally and take real responsibility for themself.

Detaching with love starts with you. You must truly convince yourself that you are not responsible for another person's disorder or their recovery from it—even if that person is your child. Of course, you will try to get them in treatment, especially a child. Naturally, if your child is under eighteen, you will have to use common sense to decide what actions to take. But no matter how old your loved one is, you do not have to let them see you get flustered, upset, or lose control. The calmer you are and the more you can let them take responsibility, the more you will reinforce that they are capable of taking care of the problem themself.

Remember: It's Detaching "with Love"

It's important to remember the "with love" part. Detaching with love is not a matter of judging others, controlling their actions, or implying approval or disapproval. If the world were a big hardware store and someone came up to you looking for the auto parts section, you might say, "I'm sorry, but I don't work here and I don't know where the auto parts are. Perhaps someone can help you at the customer service counter." This is a good example of detaching with love. It's not snapping, "Do you see me wearing a uniform? No? Then leave me alone!"

Action Step: Learning to Detach with Love (Part One)

Think of the first name of the person from whom you would like to detach. Use the person's first name. I will use the name "Joe" as an example. Now repeat the following sentence in one of the three formats. You may repeat it out loud, or say it silently to yourself.

Format 1: "I release Joe into God's care, and Joe releases me into God's care."

Format 2: "I release Joe to the Light, and Joe releases me to the Light."

Format 3: "I release Joe to his own highest good, and Joe releases me to my own highest good."

Take about twenty seconds to concentrate on this message, and repeat the sentence several times. Some people experience an immediate sensation of inner peacefulness. If you wish to, savor the message for longer than twenty seconds. Next, in the blanks below write down the first names of other people you need to detach from. Then, for each person, say each statement, wait for about twenty seconds, then repeat it.

_____

_____

Action Step: Detachment Phrases (Part Two)

Use phrases like those below to show you care but need to place the responsibility for the problem back where it belongs. Check off the statements and responses that seem most appropriate to your situation, and memorize them. The more you practice, the easier the responses will be to use. Since you know your own situation best, at the end write some other statements and possible responses like the ones given.

- ☐ THEM: "Where did you put my wallet?"

  YOU: "I don't know where you put it. Why don't you think about where you last used it and retrace your steps from there?"

- ☐ THEM (driving in a car): "It's your fault we're lost."

  YOU (passenger): "I don't feel at fault. Let's stop at the nearest gas station and we can ask for directions."

- ☐ THEM: "I can't do this. Would you do it for me?"

  YOU: "I understand it may seem overwhelming. If you break up the task into smaller pieces, it will look a whole lot more manageable."

- ☐ THEM: "There's no way I'm going to take responsibility for this! If you hadn't [done such and such], this never would have happened!"

  YOU: "I don't feel responsible, but either way, arguing is not going to solve this problem. Perhaps if we [do such and such] this problem can be solved."

- ☐ THEM "I can't do what I told you I'd do. Something else has come up."

  YOU: "I can see your dilemma. But you promised me you would do this last Tuesday, and I expect you to keep your promise."

Think about negative things your loved one member says to you and write down a non-reactive response based on the above model.

THEM: _____

_____

YOU: _____

_____

THEM: _____

_____

YOU: _____

_____

New Skills Replace Older Ones

Once you decide to take control of your own life, your primary goal will be different. Instead of walking on eggshells trying to please your loved one, you will walk on firm ground and try to please yourself. You too can replace old habits with new coping skills.

First, you should concentrate on this thought:

Differences of opinion are all right, and everyone has a right to their own opinion, including me and my loved one. Since everything is black or white to them, you may have lost sight of this fact. But its ramifications are powerful. Both you and your loved one have the right to hold your own opinions about everything, from the existence of God to how often the bathroom should be cleaned. This means that you don't have to make them believe your "truth," and vice versa. You can agree to disagree.

Action Step: It's Okay to Disagree

In this exercise, you're going to test the theory that it's okay to disagree. You will need to find a partner, preferably a friend who grew up in a family that allowed for dissenting opinions, someone who's comfortable with themself and who they are. You can choose someone you don't know that well, but be sure to choose someone who is non-threatening.

Now, come up with a topic you and your loved one disagree on. Here are some sample opinions and a space to write in your own:

- "I think the Three Stooges are greatly underrated comic actors."

  _____

  _____

- "Golf is a boring sport."

  _____

  _____

- "You should always leave a tip for the waiter, even if the service is bad."

  _____

  _____

- "I think that in 20 years, Donald Trump will be heralded as one of our greatest presidents."

  _____

  _____

- "I've always thought there's just not enough sex and violence on television."

  _____

  _____

Now, try asserting one of these opinions when you're with your friend or acquaintance. A chance may come up spontaneously. Take note of how they react. If they get huffy, just smile and say, "That's my opinion. What's yours?" If they laugh or say whatever is on their mind, relax. This is how things are supposed to happen. Next, try another statement—a harder one if the first one went well, a softer one if the first one did not.

The point of this Action Step is for you to feel comfortable giving a dissenting opinion among people who generally respect everyone's right to have their own opinion. Try this Action Step often, varying it every once in a while. For example, do something your loved one would never approve of or leave you time for. *Make* the time and do it with joy. Practice independent thinking and behaving as often as you can, even if it's choosing a different brand of ice cream. Keep track of your progress in your notebook. It should become easier and more fun over time.

Action Step: Your Mental (or Actual) Vacation

The best way to gain some clarity in your life is to take a mental—or physical, if possible—break away from your loved one. I have seen it work miracles dozens of times: people stepping out of the land of Oz and regaining their perspective on themself and their situation. Whether your break is physical, mental, or both, the point is not to think about your loved one this time, but simply have fun with people who like and support you and do not easily take offense. Remember that your loved one does not need to agree with you that you deserve this time off. If they fall into a rage, leave. It is okay for you to have a different opinion and make the decision to act in your best interest. They may not see it now, but your choice is good for them too because it makes them less dependent on you.

During this time, relax and forget about maintaining limits, speaking in exact ways, and walking on eggshells. Don't nurse any wounds, hold any grudges, or let sorrow spoil this time. Remember you're taking a vacation away from issues and problems involving your loved one.

I can't tell you exactly how to customize this for your life. But it is absolutely vital that you take a holiday away from the work associated with having someone in your life with BPD or NPD. What you do, of course, depends on the type of relationship you have and the particulars of your own situation.

The mother of a borderline son talks about taking a "mental vacation": *I do a sport called endurance riding, which is going fifty miles on a horse. It's a team event, and you and the horse have to be in shape. During the ride, I have to be completely attuned to the horse—is it lame or dehydrated? Does it need a rest? I'm outside, in beautiful country I can't get to any other way. When I ride, I can't think about my borderline child at all. It is totally absorbing. The mental vacation keeps me sane.*

Here is how one man took an actual vacation from his wife with BPD: *I went to a gathering of people with borderline spouses like me. For three days, we ate, laughed, talked, sat by a campfire, and shared stories. I didn't have to worry about walking on eggshells. No one blamed or criticized me for anything. I realized just how abnormal my life has become and what it is like to have fun again. Most of all, I felt validated because everyone there is going through the same thing. They really understood. That three days changed my life.*

Use the lines below (or in your notebook) to describe your activity and how you felt during or after it. Try this Action Step often and you will become more comfortable with it. Do it until you're positively, absolutely sure that the world doesn't end when you say or do something that displeases the great and powerful Oz, who, after all, is just a regular person behind a curtain.

Depending on your particular situation, it may be difficult to arrange this Action Step. Do it anyway, even if you have to tell a white lie to get some time to yourself. People who live with someone with BPD or NPD soon become like a fish in water: They can't describe what their world is like because they have no other perspective.

_____

_____

_____

_____

_____

_____

_____

Action Step: Because I Say So!

In Beverly Engel's book *Loving Him Without Losing You: Seven Empowering Strategies for Better Relationships* (2000), I found this quote by a woman named Liana Cordes: "I have listened to everyone else's truth and tried to make it mine. Now I am listening deep inside my own voice and I am softly, yet firmly, speaking my truth" (197). That's what this Action Step was about—finding your own voice and speaking your own truth. You have been listening to everyone else's truth and it's time to begin to listen to and trust the healthy voice inside yourself.

In the wonderful Mexican film *Like Water for Chocolate* (1992), set in the late 1800s, the mother, Elena, treats her youngest adult daughter, Tita, like a servant. She even refuses to let Tita marry, expecting her daughter to stay at home and take care of her until she dies of old age. Meanwhile, Mama Elena gives the two older sisters as much love as she can muster—and cruelly arranges the marriage of Tita's beloved to her eldest daughter, Rosaura, commanding Tita to make the wedding cake and forbidding her to cry. Later in the film, Mama Elena is killed. Even then, she comes back as a ghost and haunts her Cinderella-like daughter with the same barbs and abuse she showered on her when she was living. Finally, the daughter gains strength and tells her abusive ghost mother to go away and to never come back, and that she will not accept her mother's abuse from the Beyond any longer. It works. When Tita speaks her truth—even to a ghost abuser—it banishes her.

Was Elena really a ghost, or did she represent Tita's own self-recriminations, the way people who have been abused continue to abuse themselves after the abuser is no longer there? It doesn't matter. What matters is that you have more power than you think you do. No one can get inside your mind and force you to accept abuse. Take care that you don't become your own abuser by putting yourself down, either out loud or in your mind.

Try looking at yourself the way the people who love you see you. Ask them to write it down for you, if you're comfortable with that. Then, write a letter to yourself about all the things you like about the new you. Let go of old scripts you don't need anymore. You are the screenwriter of your own life.

_____

_____

_____

_____

_____

_____

_____

_____

_____

_____

Action Step: Frankie Says Relax

One mother of a borderline adult child said it all when she made this remark. "We do what we can. Then we do the dishes." Yes, life does go on despite the problems in your relationship, their painful feelings, and your ambivalence, worry, and chaos. This relaxation Action Step is a basic building block for some of the later Action Steps in this book. Paying attention to the feelings in your body is an important skill, and you will need to draw on it later. This exercise will work best if you record the script that follows and play it back to yourself.

Relaxation Exercise Instructions

Find a comfortable place to sit where you will not be disturbed for about twenty to thirty minutes. Sit up with your back straight, but not rigid. Keep your legs and ankles straight in front of you and uncrossed. Keeping your mind blank, close your eyes and picture a blue sky with a fluffy white cloud. As thoughts drift in, just let them drift out. Yawn and stretch. Take a deep breath and hold it, then reach your arms out at an angle over your head so that they make the shape of the letter "Y." As you hold your arms up and out, clench both fists and flex your wrists. Relax and lower your hands to your lap. Take a slow, gentle, deep breath and let it out gradually. Repeat the yawn and stretch a second time, then a third. You may be starting to feel some loosening in your muscles. It's okay if you start thinking about your loved one; it's understandable. Let the thought go. The more you practice, the better your life will be.

Now pay attention to the various muscle groups in your body. Begin with your feet. Notice how they feel—warm or cool, tense or relaxed. Tense the muscles in your feet and hold that tension for three to five seconds, then relax. Move your attention up to the calves of your legs. Notice how they feel—warm or cool, tense or relaxed. Hold the muscles tight and for three to five seconds, then shake them out. Do the same with the rest of your body, including your thigh muscles, buttocks, your lower back and abdomen, chest and upper back area, both shoulders, neck, jaw, and forehead. Hold the tension for three to five seconds, then slowly relax. Gradually take a few deep belly breaths; let your breath out slowly. Imagine that the stiffness is leaving your body each time you exhale. You may be starting to feel warm and relaxed throughout your whole body. Enjoy the feeling. You deserve it. Deeply breathe again, and as you exhale let go of all the remaining tension in your whole body.

Your whole body is now entering a state of warm, deep relaxation. Keep breathing slowly and naturally, in and out, and keep your muscles loose. Now imagine that you are lying on a beach somewhere, soaking up the warm summer sun. You can hear the distant sounds of waves crashing against the shore in the background. You can even hear seagulls crying in the distance. You feel the warmth of the sunlight penetrating your body, and you enjoy the feeling it brings to your muscles and bones, even to the marrow inside your bones. You can visualize the golden rays of sunlight as they penetrate your body. The warm, soothing rays heal you from the inside out, calming and reenergizing every part that they touch.

Now pretend that you're growing lighter because you've released so much tension. You're drifting upward like a wisp of fog toward the sun's healing touch. The sunlight caresses your body and you feel calm and tender, without a care in the world. This is what you deserve, so enjoy it to the fullest.

Whenever you are ready, you may begin drifting slowly back down to the place where you sat at the beginning of this exercise. Move slowly and lightly, like a cloud drifting down. Take a slow, deep breath and slowly let it out. As you come back, the calmness and healing light stays within you. Notice how your body feels against whatever you are sitting on; the sensations of pressure against your body. Savor the feeling and smell the clean air and feel the breeze touch your skin and soothe the muscles underneath. Notice the sounds around you.

Take another deep breath and release it slowly. Now you are fully back into the present, rested and reenergized. Stretch your arms up and out, taking another deep breath; stretch and yawn. Relax your arms and bring them back down into your lap. Look around you and notice where you are. You are fully back to your starting point, with the difference that you feel the healing inner light relaxing you from within.

One habit that people tend to fall into is forgetting about their own feelings. Although it is true that you need certain factual information to deal with BPD or NPD, you will also need the information that comes directly from your feelings. In chapter 8, for instance, you will learn how to recognize when you are being manipulated by fear, obligation, and guilt. One of your main tools for recognizing manipulation is simply noticing how your body feels at any given time. Sometimes your education and intellect will tell you the things you need to know about dealing with BPD or NPD, but at other times you cannot replace the information that comes only from your body. Once you know how your body feels when you are fully relaxed, you'll be able to detect any changes. Your body may even warn you of impending trouble before your brain does.

In this chapter, we started you on the path of self-determination with some examples of how you can assert yourself. In the next chapter, we will show you how to start treasuring the most important person in your life—you.

Reflection

After reading this chapter, what stands out to you?

_____

_____

_____

_____

_____

_____

_____

_____

_____

What have you learned in this chapter that you want to put into action?

_____

_____

_____

_____

_____

_____

_____

_____

_____

CHAPTER 6

Treasuring Yourself: Owning Your Own Reality

When we let ourselves be defined in our own minds by our worst moments instead of our best ones, we learn to think of ourselves as people who never get it right, rather than as capable people who make an occasional, thoroughly human mistake.

—Rabbi Harold Kushner

The goal of every contestant on a reality game show is the same—to outlast everyone else and win the cash. But to do that, contestants must accomplish two opposing goals: First, get rid of their competition, and second, be well-liked enough to obtain the competition's winning vote.

Like all television, reality TV shows have only one purpose: to draw an audience of people for advertisers. But as a writer of self-help books, I see them as fascinating sociology and psychology experiments. One day it hit me that, despite their different strategies, most of the winners on the shows had one thing in common: From the very beginning, they acted with the confidence and leadership of someone who had already won. Some of the winners even predicted at the outset they would outlast the competition.

Beliefs Create Your Reality

You might think that the winner's early confidence would convince other contestants to get rid of this contestant as quickly as possible. But the other contestants didn't, or couldn't. The winners—even the unlikable ones—seemed to have a presence that helped them win.

So what does this have to do with you? Everything. You may not be willing to eat bugs for money or be locked inside a house with a bunch of strangers. But the same principle applies: *The way you view yourself will compel others to treat you accordingly.* If you feel like you're a loser, you will come across as a loser and people may treat you that way. If you see yourself as a confident, worthy person (or do a good job of pretending you feel that way), people will sense it and treat you accordingly.

How Beliefs Create Reality

The way you view yourself is but one of your "realities"; every choice you make in life comes from a point of view you have learned over time—what other people, situations, and life events have taught you about yourself and your place in the world. All too often, people have come to the conclusion that they are undeserving, their choices are limited, and they are definitely not winners in the game of life. But as we grow up, we can learn to change that view.

Josh's Reality

Let me give you an example. Joshua is a thirty-five-year-old man married to Joan. Joan and Joshua have put a great deal of thought into financial planning. They bought an inexpensive house and paid it off in ten years. They've purchased used but well-maintained cars with cash. They have placed the maximum they can into retirement accounts.

But Josh's brother, Ken, lives from paycheck to paycheck. Ken, his wife, and his kids are overextended and maxed out financially. Ken drifts from job to job, blaming obnoxious bosses and impossible clients for his job-hopping. They spend first, pay later.

One day Ken calls his brother and asks for a $2,500 loan "just for a few months" because he knows Josh has a large savings account. Ken promises to pay it back, but Josh knows the real chances of that are slim. But, he ponders, what choice does he have? He and Joan have no kids or monthly payments. His brother is counting on him, and if he doesn't agree to loan Ken the money, his parents will call him "selfish" for "putting money over family." Although Joan and Josh are generous, their thrifty habits have already earned them the informal title of "Mr. and Mrs. Scrooge."

Joan's Reality

Josh's reality is that he has no choice. But his wife Joan, who comes from a family where personal limits were respected, doesn't see it that way at all. "Your brother *chose* to overspend and job-hop," she said. "Why should we reinforce his irresponsibility by bailing him out? Maybe it's a lesson he needs to learn and by giving him money we're not really doing him a favor."

"What am I supposed to do, watch my brother starve?" Joshua retorts.

"I don't think he'll starve," Joan says. "This is not a matter of life or death. This is a matter of giving up ballet lessons, a housekeeper, and cable TV."

In this scenario, Josh didn't want to earn his family's animosity. But since it was Joan's money, too, he had to say "no" to his brother. Just as he thought, Ken put up a fuss. But Joan's prediction also came true. Ken and his family were not forced onto the streets and did not subsist on peanut butter and jelly. Instead, Josh's parents bailed him out by getting a cash advance from their credit card (at 18 percent interest). And sure enough, Ken still hasn't paid it back. Still, Josh had to endure some discomfort when he "went against his family."

Lessons Learned

Although Joan was glad that they didn't get stuck with Ken's debts, she was unhappy that Josh had used her as the sole reason for the loan's decline. But she knew it was difficult for him to balance his needs with the needs of his family.

Josh and Joan told this story at a retreat for family members of an HCP, and several of us were trying to make Josh comprehend that as long as Ken knew he had a free ride, he wasn't going to change. We weren't getting through to Josh until out of frustration I whipped out my wallet and started handing dollar bills to him. "Do you want more?" I asked, filling his palm with cash. After a minute or two, confused, he said, "Stop."

Then another member of the group yelled, "I'll take the money!" and I turned and continued putting bills into someone else's palm until I was finally down to my credit cards. Finally, Josh got the message: Ken would keep asking for money, going from crisis to crisis, as long as the money river flowed freely. More importantly, Josh finally caught on that since it was his money, he got to choose what to do with it.

"But what about the pressure from my family?" he asked.

"What about it?" I responded. "Are they going to call the police and report you for refusing to give someone a loan?"

He thought for a moment. "I'm forty years old. I don't need my family's approval."

"Bingo," I said.

Who Determines Your Reality?

Most people with an HCP in their life have been invalidated for so long that if you told them the sky was green, they'd believe it. A group of them from Moving Forward once got together in Wisconsin, where I live. Since I don't like cigarette smoke, I joked that by law, smoking was not permitted anywhere in the entire state of Wisconsin. I never imagined that anyone would take my comment seriously. But a smoker with a mother and ex-husband with BPD nearly canceled her trip until I convinced her that no such law existed. Some restaurants and buildings banned smoking, yes. But how could they ban it everywhere in the entire state? She was relieved to know it was a joke.

So where is your reality coming from? From the HCP in your life? From your parents? Your partner? If you're like most non-BPs, you have a difficult time listening to yourself and believing your own perceptions. It's one of the reasons you're using this workbook. Confidently forming your own opinion is one way of treasuring yourself. You have just as much right to do this as anyone else.

Action Step: Are You a Disappearing Person?

Author Beverly Engel (2000) shows how early influences set up some people to be what she calls "disappearing people." In a relationship, a "disappearing person" gives up part of themselves in order for the relationship to continue. Engel's book is not about BPD or NPD, but from my experience, some of its lessons are valuable for people in your situation. I have adapted this questionnaire from Engel's book to help you identify if you are a "disappearing person." Answer the following question with a "yes" or "no" based on your first, intuitive response:

1. **Y N** Is there an implicit agreement that your loved one's views are somehow "better" or more valid?

2. **Y N** When a compromise needs to be made, are you usually the one making it?

3. **Y N** Are you afraid to assert yourself because you're afraid you'll lose the other person's approval, friendliness, or the relationship itself?

4. **Y N** Have you stopped doing things you used to enjoy to keep this relationship?

5. **Y N** If the HCP in your life is your child, have you let your child's problems outweigh the rest of your family's needs? Your own needs? Their siblings needs?

6. **Y N** If your person is a new partner, did the relationship seem to come together very quickly and passionately? Do you spend most of your time daydreaming about this person?

7. **Y N** If your person is a longtime partner, have you forgotten what a "normal" relationship is like?

8. **Y N** If your loved one is a parent, do you still feel you need their approval even though you're past age eighteen? If you answered "no," are you afraid of disclosing important parts of your life you know would meet with disapproval?

9. **Y N** Do you question or devalue your own interpretation of events or opinions when they differ from your loved one's?

10. **Y N** Are you being dishonest by omitting crucial information or directly telling untruths in this relationship?

11. **Y N** Do you wonder why you keep up this relationship even though it's almost all negative?

12. **Y N** Do you feel what you bring to the relationship is valued and acknowledged?

13. **Y N** Does this relationship keep you so occupied it doesn't leave much time for your own growth as a person?

14. **Y N** Does this relationship keep you so occupied that you don't have time to work on your own problems because their needs come first?

No matter the type of relationship, you have the right to be respected and treated with kindness. If the majority of your answers just now showed a lack of respect for yourself, your opinions, wants, and beliefs, you may be a disappearing person—especially if you are the adult child of an HCP. But you can change this, and this chapter will show you how.

Action Step: Why Do You Disappear?

The next step is identifying where you learned your role in the HCP "dance," to give you insight into why you are giving away pieces of yourself in this relationship. Again, I adapted the following questionnaire from Engel (2000).

Answer the following questions "yes" or "no." If the answer is "yes," rate the intensity of the problem from 1 to 3, with a 3 being the most intense. Base your answer on your *perception* of the problem. For example, perhaps your parent was absent for a time due to being deployed with the military. But as a child, you may not have been able to understand that and processed the information as "my parent abandoned me."

Do you feel that you had trouble bonding well with your parents?

Y N   Rating _____

Were one or both of your parents absent for a long time during your childhood—either away entirely because of divorce or abandonment, work or other preoccupations, alcoholism or substance abuse, or because they were emotionally absent?

Y N   Rating _____

Were your needs neglected, either physically or emotionally?

Y N   Rating _____

Did your parents minimize, oppose, or make fun of your needs?

Y N   Rating _____

Were you physically or sexually abused by anyone, or forced to watch someone else being abused? This includes inappropriate touching, discussion, or sexual "joking" you could not control or understand.

Y N   Rating _____

Were you verbally or emotionally abused or repeatedly exposed to abuse?

Y N   Rating _____

Were you rejected or ridiculed by your parents, siblings, peers, or community?

Y N   Rating _____

Did you fantasize about killing yourself or murdering another person?

Y N   Rating _____

Did you cope with childhood pain by constantly "numbing out," going into a shell and trying to ignore or repress the pain?

Y N   Rating _____

Was your childhood cut short because you were expected to serve as chief caretaker for someone else, such as an alcoholic parent or younger siblings? Or, were you expected to take on other adult responsibilities (such as working in the family business) when most children your age were enjoying a carefree life?

Y N   Rating _____

Answering "yes" to any of the questions above puts you at risk of being a disappearing person. But like a magician creating an illusion, you haven't really disappeared. The real you is there, just submerged and waiting for you to discover and unearth the treasures within.

Learning to Love Yourself

It's no secret that relationships take work. It takes time to get to know another person. Misunderstandings are common. So are fights. At times, you will need to forgive the other person if they did not mean to hurt you or sincerely regret doing so.

Forming a relationship with yourself is just as challenging—even more so because it's not as supported in our society. If you don't know yourself—or aren't particularly friendly with the you within—you'll need more than this workbook to truly work on treasuring yourself. If you're the adult child of an HCP, chances are very high you need to give yourself the unconditional love you didn't get as a child. While other people can offer friendship and more, they cannot substitute for self-love.

Living the Treasured Life

I've read many books on personal limits and boundaries. But the best by far is the revolutionary book *Better Boundaries: Owning and Treasuring Your Own Life* by Jan Black and Greg Enns (1998). While most books of this type concentrate on the mechanics of setting, communicating, and observing limits, Black and Enns understand that the key to boundaries is not technical, but rather a natural outgrowth of your beliefs about how you deserve to be treated. If you are in a relationship with an HCP who is foisting their own self-loathing onto you in some way, neither you nor the relationship will survive unless you truly love yourself and treat yourself accordingly. In the absence of self-love, you will continue to let the HCP control your life. In the presence of self-love, your limits will flow from your conviction that you deserve to be treated with respect. This next three-part Action Step was inspired by this understanding.

Action Step: Treasuring Yourself (Part One)

This Action Step is designed to reach you on an emotional level. Pick a quiet, private time when you're alone, don't feel pressured, and aren't preoccupied with other things going on in your life.

Imagine for a moment that you are walking through the parking lot in front of a busy grocery store on a bright, sunny day. As you near the store entrance, you see a car parked directly in the sun with a child sleeping in the front seat. You are already feeling the heat and perspiring. It dawns on you that it must be terribly hot in that car, and that the toddler must be badly overheated and maybe even unconscious.

You quickly look around for the owner and try to open the door. But the car is locked, no windows are open, and you're the only one who can see what's going on. Everyone else is busy with their groceries, the owner of the car is out of sight—probably one of 150 people in the store—and you know that within minutes, the child could die or be seriously injured—if they are not already. Check off the emotions that describe what you're feeling (not thinking) in the spaces below, and add other feelings in the blanks provided. An emotion is one word. Sad, happy, lost. If you say a phrase, write it down until you come to a feeling.

☐ Scared	☐ Happy	☐ Unconcerned
☐ Angry	☐ Guilty	☐ _____
☐ Worried	☐ Frantic	☐ _____
☐ Stressed	☐ Numb	☐ _____
☐ Helpless	☐ Desperate	

Now, what do you do, if anything? Fill in an alternative response, if you have one, in the blank space provided.

☐ Start yelling for help _____

_____

☐ Take something heavy—your shoe, a nearby rock—and break the window farthest from the baby, reach in, and unlock the door

_____

_____

☐ Run inside the store, find the manager, and ask them to make an announcement

_____

_____

☐ Shrug your shoulders, walk inside the store, and start looking for your favorite brand of cereal

_____

_____

☐ _____

_____

_____

☐ _____

_____

_____

☐ _____

_____

_____

Action Step: Treasuring Yourself (Part Two)

If you're like most people, you would go to great lengths to prevent the child from being hurt. You would probably be angry at the caregiver who left the child alone in the car. And if it was the parents who left the child in the car (as opposed to a babysitter), you'd probably worry about how the child was being cared for at home. You may muster a great deal of indignation when people you care about are treated unfairly or abused. I see it every day on the internet. But when the people in those groups themselves become the objects of verbal or emotional abuse, they don't see it, they try to brush it off, they vainly hope things will improve, or they even blame themselves.

That's why now I'd like you to imagine that *you* were the child inside that car—an innocent child, too young to make mistakes—whose life or death was at the mercy of the adults around them. You once *were* that child, self-centered, unspoiled, and unaware of anything but your own immediate needs. Please look at the example and respond with a gut-level reaction. The questions are not meant to be taken literally, but metaphorically and emotionally. You may get more in touch with your feelings if you try writing with your non-dominant hand.

How did it feel to be trapped inside the car? Example: *I cried when I thought of the little me alone, with no one to help me and my parents out somewhere, not even seeing that I am hurting.*

_____

_____

_____

_____

Where were your parents? Who left you there? Example: *My dad left me alone with my mother. I don't know where he is. She needed something in the store. She normally does fine with my physical needs, but she needed something and never considered the dangers of leaving me alone and how it might affect me later in life.*

_____

_____

_____

_____

_____

Did you do anything to deserve what happened to you? Example: *Of course not. Maybe. Maybe I wasn't the baby they wanted. For some reason, I wasn't good enough and I don't know why.*

_____

_____

_____

_____

What happened to you in the car? Write the ending to the scenario. Example: *The lady who found me thought about making a fuss, but she was too busy. A few more people walked by. One of them was concerned, but didn't think it was her place to help. When my mother got back, she didn't even notice how hot it was in the car for me. Now I have some kind of damage and I am even more flawed than before. When I grow up, I will be marked, but I won't remember the incident, because I was too young when it happened. It will be just another mystery as to why I'm not "normal."*

_____

_____

_____

_____

Action Step: Treasuring Yourself (Part Three)

Now I'd like you to imagine again that the baby in the car is you as a child, which I'll refer to as the Child You. The worried woman outside of the car is the Adult You. The Adult You has the ability and desire to change the ending so that the Child You is taken care of, not just that day but every day. This lets you be the parent to yourself that you always wanted. Answer the following questions.

What does the Adult You do to protect the baby inside?

_____

_____

_____

_____

_____

_____

What does the Adult You say to the caretaker(s) when you finally meet them?

_____

_____

_____

_____

_____

_____

Imagine that the Child You grows up a bit and can now react to people, situations, and events with raw, primary emotions. How do they feel? What do they want?

_____

_____

_____

_____

_____

_____

How can the Adult You help the child within?

_____

_____

_____

_____

_____

_____

_____

In your life, there will be people who disappoint you, friends who leave you, coworkers who betray you, and relatives who don't really know who you are. Find a place where you can be quiet and alone (bring a box of tissues) and say the following sentences out loud from the Adult You to the Child You. Say them several times—the Child You has been betrayed and needs some encouragement to learn to trust. They have been waiting a long time to hear these words, and may feel guarded. The Adult You needs to be patient.

In the spaces provided, write the Child You's response. Use your notebook if you need more room.

I will always be there for you. I pledge to treat you gently and with kindness, even if others don't.

_____

_____

_____

_____

_____

I will always love you. You are the most special person to me in the whole world.

_____

_____

_____

_____

_____

I will not abandon you, no matter what. You will always be safe and protected with me.

_____

_____

_____

_____

No matter what you've done in the past, I forgive you. You did the best you could, always, with the tools you had at the time. Each new day I will love and forgive you a little more.

_____

_____

_____

_____

_____

Take a break now and sit with those feelings, and come back to the rest of this chapter later.

Action Step: What Do Other People Think of Me?

Now, looking at the following list of qualities, what messages did you incorporate as you grew up? Where did they come from? Think about your peers, relatives, community, significant events, parents, babysitters, teachers, media, and so on. The first one serves as an example. Add other traits, and where you got these messages, in the space provided at the end.

I would describe myself as:

Example:

☐ Attractive/unattractive *I have a nice face, but could stand to lose weight.*

I got this message from *my mother.*

☐ Attractive/unattractive _____

I got this message from _____

☐ Powerful/powerless _____

I got this message from _____

☐ Perfect/flawed _____

I got this message from _____

☐ Competent/incompetent _____

  I got this message from _____

☐ Extroverted/introverted _____

  I got this message from _____

☐ Mentally healthy/crazy _____

  I got this message from _____

☐ Timid/bossy _____

  I got this message from _____

☐ Lovable/unlovable _____

  I got this message from _____

☐ Smart/stupid _____

  I got this message from _____

☐ Selfless/selfish _____

  I got this message from _____

☐ Sensible/foolish _____

  I got this message from _____

☐ Thrifty/spendthrift _____

  I got this message from _____

☐ Successful/failure _____

  I got this message from _____

☐ Coordinated/uncoordinated _____

  I got this message from _____

☐ Talented/untalented _____

I got this message from _____

☐ Witty/dull _____

I got this message from _____

☐ Successful/underachieving _____

I got this message from _____

Now that you've looked at the messages you've received from the outside, go on to examine them critically in the next Action Step.

Action Step: What Do I Think of Me?

Look at your answers to the previous Action Step. Ask yourself these questions and record your answers in your notebook.

- Is this opinion someone else's that I've absorbed without really knowing if it's true?

- Is this an old statement that was true but no longer fits?

- What evidence or examples am I using for these opinions? Is the source one I can trust to have my best interests in mind?

- Am I overemphasizing my mistakes and discounting the times when things go right? Or, am I taking one or two examples and giving them too much weight?

- Am I playing the game "Feelings Equal Facts" (I feel useless so I must be useless)?

- Am I blaming myself for problems that have complicated causes (e.g., arguments or problems with my loved one, labels leftover from my childhood)?

Many people who were unpopular or unhappy in high school say they still think of themselves in the same way they were stereotyped in school. Similarly, people who get labeled, fairly or unfairly, by their family may later have trouble shaking these labels, especially when they're around the very people who came up with them. Even if a negative trait rang true, would a loving friend or family member point to it? Or would they stress your positive qualities? How do you define yourself? Are you defining yourself by your positive qualities or by those you would like to change? Do you spend time with people who see and comment on your positive qualities or do you spend time with people who consistently remind you of your mistakes—perhaps to make themselves feel better? A person who treasures themself will spend the most time with people who treasure them.

Ways to Boost Your Self-Worth

Black and Enns (1998) offer several innovative ways to help people develop better self-esteem. I've adapted some of their suggestions for this workbook. Check off the ones that look the most effective for you. In the lines following, make note of how you might incorporate it into your life.

☐ Forgive yourself for all misdeeds, real or imagined. In order to forgive yourself, you may need to acknowledge that you feel flawed—perhaps because when you were a child your primary caretakers were not able to give you all that you needed. It doesn't mean they woke up every day asking themselves how they could ruin your self-worth. The truth is that you are a better person than they ever thought they could produce. We can be our own worst critics, berating ourselves for past mistakes others never knew or forgot years ago. (If you still can't practice self-forgiveness, I strongly suggest outside professional help.)

_____

_____

☐ Get to know your preferences in food, hobbies, and other areas as you would those of a new friend. If you weren't given many choices growing up, now is the time to experiment. The film *City of Angels* is about a character who can't touch, taste, smell, or have many experiences we all take for granted. It is a good movie to watch when you take what you have for granted and need to be reminded what a treasure it is to be alive with the free will to determine your own fate.

_____

_____

☐ Make choices that show that you treasure yourself. This could include everything from seeing a doctor on a regular basis to changing jobs.

_____

_____

☐ Learn to trust yourself. Listen to your intuition. Don't let anyone intimidate or fool you. Most people in chosen relationships with an HCP say they feel a sense that all is not right, but they choose to ignore it because they want to believe in the "perfection" they thought they found.

_____

_____

☐ Accept the parts of yourself that you don't like and can't change. Does anyone really care that you're not taller? Or, if you can change something and it plays an important role in your self-image, work on it. If it would make you feel better about yourself to learn to drive, take lessons even if it scares you. When you become self-critical, determine if this is a real issue or a false one.

_____

_____

☐ When you have a hard time making good choices, pretend that you're making them for someone you love. If you're angry and have a choice between eating a pint of gourmet ice cream and taking a long walk, pretend you're someone you love and ask yourself what advice you would give that person.

_____

_____

☐ If you're feeling fear or awkwardness in a situation, feel your feeling and then power through and do what you need to do anyway—go to a party where you don't know many people, join a new church, or give a toast at a wedding. One year, I invited everyone from my Moving Forward online support group to come to my house. I had only met a few members. Only a few of them had met me. But people traveled from all over the country to be with other people they had been corresponding with for a year. For most, it meant leaving their loved one for a weekend and going to a strange place to be with people they had never met. Yet fifty people made the trip. One woman walked into the house and immediately started crying because it was so emotional for her. Another woman came from Canada just a few weeks after her daughter died, so she could be with people who had supported her through the daughter's long illness. For those who wonder about the wisdom of inviting fifty people you don't know to your house, I'm happy to tell you that the day after the party, a volunteer cleanup crew straightened up the whole house, including mopping the kitchen floor.

_____

_____

☐ When you are engaging in self-defeating thinking, become conscious of it, tell yourself to stop, and start thinking about something positive. Become aware of your own self-talk. Are you a silent verbal abuser of yourself?

_____

_____

☐ Decorate your home and work with images, such as photographs, that remind you of ways that you treasure yourself, or other objects that remind you of something important (such as a collection of keys to represent boundaries).

_____

_____

☐ Collect positive sources of inspiration, such as cards, verses, poetry, letters, and notes from others that charge your spirit or remind you that others cherish you.

_____

_____

☐ Visualize your goal, whether it be concrete (learning a sport) or not (learning to love yourself). Professional athletes have coaches who train them to do this. It's just as important for the rest of us.

_____

_____

☐ Counter resisting thoughts, such as "I can't change," or criticism from others, with innovative ideas.

_____

_____

☐ Make it easy to attain your goals by making sure the tools for change (e.g., your walking shoes) are within easy reach all the time.

_____

_____

Personal Limits and Treasuring Yourself

This section is applicable when your HCP is an adult or older teenager. If your loved one is a child, you may need different tools that are wrapped up in child raising. To learn about that, read the book _Stop Walking on Eggshells for Parents._ If you want to learn tools specific to partners, also read _Stop Walking on Eggshells for Partners._

When discussing personal limits or boundaries with people who have an HCP loved one, I am often amazed at how many people don't believe they have a right to set limits, don't know what their limits are, have no idea what to do if someone pushes their boundaries, and are in general uncomfortable with the whole idea. The word "boundary" especially seems to bother some people—even though it's a personal limit by another name. "Personal limit" sounds less threatening and I suggest you use this language. Even the best relationships have boundaries. If you feel guilty for having your own needs or desires, you may want to consider a therapist. These feelings can stem from a childhood in which the more you gave up, the more you were loved.

You should develop limits based on what feels good to you. Again, if you have a hard time visualizing how to set limits, imagine doing it for a friend of yours. Think of how you would like your best friend to be treated. Then treat yourself that way.

Setting Limits Around Emotional and Verbal Abuse

No one—let me repeat, no one—deserves to be abused in any way. What is abuse? Whatever feels abusive to you. Whatever makes you want to walk away. Whatever makes you cry or feels uncomfortable. You may want to see if other people find a certain behavior acceptable or unacceptable. Conducting reality checks is necessary for many people. But ultimately you have to decide. Even if ninety-nine out of a hundred people wouldn't mind their friend's children calling them by their first name, *you* may wish to be called Mr. or Ms. So-and-So.

The following are some small steps in the right direction:

1. Truly believe you have a right to set reasonable limits. Read literature on the subject for more information.

2. Remind yourself that setting personal limits benefits everyone: both you and others, especially HCPs. Limits make the relationship healthier and last longer with fewer arguments if you are firm about them.

3. When setting limits, try using the DEAR technique described below. The technique was designed by Marsha Linehan, PhD, especially for people with borderline personality disorder (1993). It's simple and can be used with anyone, not just people with BPD. The key is to practice with your friends and family.

Action Step: Using DEAR in Real Life

Now is the time to examine the index cards that you created in chapter 4. As you may recall, these cards contain qualities you would like to have in your relationship. Take them out and read through them, making sure they're up to date. Then choose something that your loved one can do (or not do) if they choose. One way to tell is to ask yourself if you have seen them extend a certain courtesy to other people they don't know as well as they know you. If your loved one is a smoker and can spend a few hours not smoking around friends who can't stand smoke, there's no reason why they can't give the same courtesy to you. In addition, pick something that is a lower priority and is one of the simpler, easy-to-follow limits. You want to be successful, so start small. Write down your limit here:

_____

_____

_____

_____

_____

When you talk to your loved one:

1. *Describe* the situation as you see it without exaggerating, making judgments, or explaining how you felt about it. Be as objective and as specific as you can. It may help to pretend you are a video camera capturing the action exactly as it happened. For example, "Last night at dinner, you called me 'unfaithful in my heart' because I was watching a movie starring a beautiful actress." Do not use judgmental or loaded words or phrases. Do not claim that you are privy to their inner motivations or feelings, because you aren't. But you can say that it appeared as if they were upset, angry, etc. More examples include the following:

   "When you yell at me, I tune out what you are saying."

   "When you smoke, it really bothers me because I don't like the smell."

   "It seems like we go to a lot of horror movies. I'd like to see a Marvel movie. Can we compromise?"

   "Yesterday you didn't come home until after midnight. I was afraid you were in a car accident."

   Now describe your situation: _____

   _____

   _____

   _____

   _____

   _____

2. *Express* your feelings or opinions about the situation clearly. Take responsibility for your own feelings. (For example, do not say, "You made me feel this way.") You may need to do some thinking beforehand in order to determine your exact emotions. Try to identify what your feelings are, as opposed to feelings that the HCP may be trying to project onto you. Examples (continuing with the same limits) include the following:

> "I feel awful when you yell at me."

> "Since I've told you smoking bothers me and you still smoke, it makes me feel like you don't care."

> "I really don't like horror movies. They give me nightmares."

> "I was very worried about you."

What are your feelings? _____

_____

_____

_____

_____

3. *Assert* your limits, making them simple. Again, explain that you are setting this limit, not because it is right, expected, normal, or how your loved one should act. Instead, you want this because it is your personal preference. This ends a conversation about whether it's "normal" to want this limit. The behavior makes you feel uncomfortable, and that's all you need. It may be difficult for you to not argue. Restrain yourself. Here are some examples:

> "If you yell at me, I'm going to walk away and come back later when you're calmer so that I feel safer."

> "When you smoke around me, I'm going to have to move away to feel better. I also won't be able to get in the car with you unless you leave your cigarettes at home."

> "I won't go to any more horror movies. They're scary to me, I don't have a good time, and I would rather rent a comedy."

> "If you are going to be late, I need you to call me."

Now assert what is acceptable to you (a new limit, a compromise, etc.): _____

_____

_____

_____

_____

4. *Repeat* yourself if necessary—several times is all right—and *reinforce* the benefits of your limits. If appropriate, help them see the negative effects of the status quo and your unwillingness to continue things as they are. Here are some examples of reinforcement:

   "If I feel safer, I will feel better about our relationship, which will improve."

   "This way I'll feel better physically and mentally and we can have a better time together."

   "We can find something we both enjoy watching and have a better time."

   "You need to abide by the rules in this house if you want to live here. You're under 18 and I am responsible for you. I love you, and I need to do whatever I have to in order to keep you safe."

   Reinforce your limit: _____

   _____

   _____

   _____

In the Moving Forward support group, I have found that there are a lot of questions about how to best define your limits. I've collected some of these below.

Common Questions About Limits

1. **When is the best time to communicate about your limits?**

   When you are setting limits for the first time, make sure you have thought them through, planned for countermoves, and thought through each response. The best time is when your loved one is feeling fairly calm (or as calm as they get). Assure that you have privacy, time, and that nothing is likely to interrupt you. If you have let this limit slide before, acknowledge that fact so they don't feel invalidated. Simply explain that you don't feel good when this happens, and you've done some thinking and changed your mind about how to handle the situation.

2. **What if the HCP doesn't observe your limits?**

    Setting limits is not about changing the person's behavior, because you can't do that. Setting limits is about how you will take care of yourself when they step over your limits. For example, if they smoke, leave the house or go outside and watch the beautiful sky. Walk the dog. Do not attend the horror movie. Go to a hotel if they continually wake you up. Other options might be to move out, get a divorce or separation, send a child to a residential center, change your phone number, or avoid family functions. List the possibilities of ways you can take care of yourself:

    _____

    _____

    _____

    _____

    _____

    You will need to think this through. When you first set limits—especially if you have let them slide before, your loved one will test your resolve through "countermoves." A countermove is a limit violation that takes things one step further—for example, if they yelled at you at home and you set a personal limit on yelling, now they may yell in public. Plan for this by developing a list of ways you can take care of yourself and make them responsible for their actions.

    Many people are under the impression that the world will collapse around them if they refuse to submit to someone's abusive behavior. It's the opposite—that's when life starts to be worth living.

3. **What if they don't agree, start arguing, or change the subject?**

    Of course they're not going to agree. The most likely scenario is that they will immediately complain about you to avoid accountability, get things into safer territory, and continue to attempt to control you with their threats, emotional blackmail, and gaslighting. Say, "I hear you, and we can talk about me as soon as we're done with this conversation."

Anticipate responses from them and develop phrases to get you back on track. Remember that personal limits don't need to be explained or justified. You are a unique person who deserves to be treated with respect.

- If they try to change the subject, use the broken record technique: Repeat yourself again and again without elaborating, justifying, or backing down.

- Ignore biting or sarcastic comments meant to derail you (don't take the bait).

- Refuse to discuss whether the limit is "right" or "wrong." (It's a non-issue. It's your limit because this is what you require.)

- If someone will not respect your limits, you need to take care of yourself first.

- If this is a chosen relationship, ask yourself why you would want to be with someone who doesn't respect your limits.

4. **What if they say they did observe your limit but you know they didn't?**

- HCPs are grandmasters at forgetting or rewriting their bad behavior. If you ask, "Do you remember threatening to XXX" and they deny it, you can say, "Can I assume then that you will not threaten XXX in the future?"

- You can simply say, "I remember it differently, but I am not bringing this up to hash out the past. I'm telling you what is and is not an acceptable way for people to treat me. If you make these threats again, I will do XXX."

- If they disagree—saying, in effect, that threatening XXX is okay—you can say, adding the phrase, "These kinds of threats may be okay for you, but not for me." Assure them you are serious by explaining what you will do for yourself if it happens again.

5. **Won't limits hurt them?**

No. They help HCPs learn to deal with their emotions and needs for themselves. Someone with BPD uses others to manage their emotions, and people with NPD use people to manage their self-esteem. As long as you are their security blanket, they don't need to know how to take care of themself. That doesn't mean they are going to jump up and down for joy. It's hard work; similar to being booted out of the house because you're 42 and need to find a job and apartment.

In this chapter, I showed you a path of self-love that will make it easier for you to contend with HCP behavior. In chapter 8, I will address disarming three potent weapons in the HCP's arsenal: fear, obligation, and guilt.

Reflection

After reading this chapter, what stands out to you?

_____

_____

_____

_____

_____

_____

_____

_____

What have you learned in this chapter that you want to put into action?

_____

_____

_____

_____

_____

_____

_____

_____

CHAPTER 7

Clearing the FOG: Fear, Obligation, and Guilt

You have to create some emotional distance between you and the person you're trying to help, and you've got to do it at the moment when they need you most. If that's not one of the most annoying facts of life, I'd like to know what is.

—Linda Richman, *I'd Rather Laugh: How to Be Happy When Life Has Other Plans for You*

Since you can't change your loved one, there is only one way to change the dynamic: Change yourself. This will enable you to feel less trapped and open your eyes to the variety of options before you. For example, you can change the way you look at their behavior, you can set limits that have consequences, you can end the "blame game," or you can sell everything and move to Hawaii. If you have children, your first duty should be to protect them. If you're a parent, you need to learn new parenting skills developed to raise kids with BPD or NPD.

This chapter will help you connect your logic and emotions and teach you how to:

- Step back to see the "dance" (interaction) for what it really is. This requires you to objectively observe behavior (yours and theirs) and identify unhealthy patterns.

- Help you recognize how they are "leading" the dance and how you're following as best you can, backwards and in heels. In your case, you can act as well as react.

- Teach you how to initiate your own healthier steps—in other words, start acting in your own best interest and the best interest of the people in your life instead of just tolerating circumstances beyond your control. As an adult, you can create the circumstances that are best for you and your loved ones.

Once you learn these new "steps," you can model them for others who need help. Keep in mind that the more you spare your loved one from reaping the natural consequences of their behavior, the less likely it is that they will change. That is your power: the ability to take control of your own life, make the best choices for yourself, and let your loved one face the consequences of their own actions.

Some of the things that are most harmful to humans are invisible to the naked eye: bacteria and viruses, for example; one cancerous cell, dividing; and emotional blackmail, easily detected with training, but invisible even under a microscope.

What Is Emotional Blackmail?

According to Susan Forward, PhD (Forward and Frazier 1997), emotional blackmail is a "powerful form of manipulation in which people close to us threaten, directly or indirectly, to punish us if we don't do what they want." The main tool of the trade, Forward says, is FOG: fear, obligation, and guilt.

Your loved one may use emotional blackmail because it's the best or the only way they know how to get what they want or need (personality disorders limit the person's ability to get what they need and want). Victims capitulate and perpetrators use whatever works again and again.

FOG in Action

FOG works in the dark. It resides in the land of emotion, not logic. At the heart of it is this flawed reasoning: "It is permissible for *me* to push *your* buttons to get *my* needs met, but if *you* try the same thing, I'll make sure you will regret your selfishness."

That's right: The emotional blackmailer's reasoning is illogical; they live by a double standard. That's why emotional blackmail is never discussed outright: The minute you try to shine a light on it by bringing it up or asking pointed questions, it will scurry away like a cockroach. If you try to pin a blackmailer down—"Are you saying you will pout if I refuse to go to the party with you?"—they will project the FOG back onto you, deny its existence, or try to distract you by changing the subject, being dramatic, or getting angry. The supposed anger may have nothing to do with the particular topic—a combination of anger with a request to change the subject is designed to throw you off-balance.

How Blackmailing Works

A "FOG transaction" has four parts: the demand, the resistance, pressure and threats, and compliance.

The Demand. This can be direct (e.g., "I want custody") or indirect ("Nothing's wrong. I know you don't have time to listen to my petty relationship problems"). In the latter case, for example, your friend Sheila may call to talk about her latest fight with her boyfriend. The unspoken demand is that if you don't insist on a full accounting of the fight right now—and take her side—she will sulk and get angry.

The Resistance. In your heart, you know you don't want to play this game. You want to take a brisk walk on this beautiful day, so you ask if the discussion can wait until another day. Sheila pauses, sighs, and moans, "I guuuueeeeessss so," meaning, "I want to talk about it *now*." This may push one of your hot buttons—you feel you are a giving person who cares about your friends—and the blackmailer is counting on your image of yourself being more important than your own needs and wishes.

Pressure and threats. Depending on many factors, pressure and threats can be subtle or quite direct. Since Sheila has been a friend for a long time, she knows that you pride yourself on being kind to others. So she uses this to engage FOG. "I guess I can wait," she says, "but I really need to talk now. I feel like you did when you called me about your father's illness and I rushed right over. If you can't find time for me now, I just don't know if you're really my friend."

Compliance. You've heard this same story from Sheila dozens of times, and you know that if you keep rushing over, she'll never learn how to start dealing with disappointment on her own. Reminded of what a "good friend" the blackmailer has been, afraid Sheila might not want to be your friend if you don't talk to her, feeling a bit guilty for wanting to exercise when your friend is in misery, and not looking forward to being called "selfish," you listen to a full accounting of your friend's problems during the hour you had set aside to do something for yourself. Bingo, you've been successfully FOGged.

FOG and Its Use in Emotional Blackmail

Manipulation can take many forms. Here are some other examples:

- Grant is fully aware that his wife is having an affair with a man named Sam. He knows because she talks about him and compares them sexually. But he's afraid if he demands that she stop seeing Sam, she'll just leave him. That's *fear*.

- As an adult, Susan tries to avoid her mother Judith's rages, complaints about others, and contagious sour moods. But Susan feels compelled to call her mother back when she leaves a message. If she doesn't, eventually Judith will reach her and demand to know, "Where were you?" Judith has been living alone since her dad finally left her mother, and Susan likes to think of herself as a "good person." For her, this means that she has a tendency to put the needs of others above her own—something her mother is counting on. This is *obligation*.

- Jack and Ramona have a teenage daughter they think is borderline. She's totally out of control; normal discipline doesn't work. They don't know where she goes at night, and they're afraid she'll do something reckless and get hurt. But they just can't put their own daughter in a residential treatment center. She would hate it. Down deep, Jack and Ramona are worried that something they did caused their daughter's disorder. They feel *guilty*. Guilt does you no good when it comes to HCP relationships. They try to apply it, and unlike pressure, you do them the favor of applying it to yourself. Acknowledge the feeling and then make the best decision for yourself whether you should feel guilty.

Action Step: Rounding Up the Usual Suspects

Make a list of people in your life who try to engage you in emotional blackmail. Use your feelings as a guide: If it feels like blackmail, it probably is. Think about some situations in life in which emotional blackmailers play with your experience of fear, obligation, or guilt to manipulate you. What is it that they want from you, and how do they usually try to get it? Write down an example or two. Try to recall who said what, how you felt, and what you told yourself when you capitulated.

Action Step: DeFOGging Your Life

To deFOG your life, start by identifying places where you are vulnerable and installing FOG-alert devices. The following are examples to help you recognize the process.

Fear

"Anger seems to magnetize fear, pulling it quickly to the surface . . . for many of us, this emotion seems so dangerous that we're afraid of it in any form. And we fear not only other people's anger, but our own" (Forward and Frazier 1997, 45).

On a scale of 1 to 5, with 1 being low and 5 being high, how afraid are you of the following scenarios? Explain your fear in your notebook: Take your vague feeling and think as practically as possible. What exactly are you afraid of happening? What is your best and worst-case scenario? Be as realistic as you can.

I am afraid of:

- ☐ Losing my loved one's approval

- ☐ Getting them angry with me

- ☐ Getting the "silent treatment"

- ☐ Them getting into danger

- ☐ Them getting into legal trouble

- ☐ Them getting depressed

- ☐ Being thought of as "selfish"

- ☐ Change

- ☐ Taking responsibility

- ☐ Being found out

- ☐ Being a bad partner

- ☐ Being a bad child/parent

- ☐ Being a bad friend

- ☐ Fear of abandonment
- ☐ Fear of retaliation
- ☐ People thinking that I'm a bad person
- ☐ Trying something new
- ☐ Losing the relationship
- ☐ Loss of love/friendship/companionship
- ☐ Losing contact with or custody of my children
- ☐ Lies being told about me
- ☐ Being alone
- ☐ Living by myself
- ☐ Taking care of certain practical matters
- ☐ Being called names
- ☐ Being embarrassed in public
- ☐ Being threatened
- ☐ Being falsely arrested
- ☐ Becoming depressed
- ☐ Failing to live up to expectations
- ☐ Confrontation
- ☐ Getting angry
- ☐ Losing control

Obligation

"When our sense of obligation is stronger than our sense of self-respect and self-caring, blackmailers quickly learn how to take advantage" (Forward and Frazier 1997, 51).

On a scale of 1 to 5, how strongly do you resonate with the following statements of obligation? For each statement you rate highly, make some notes in response to the following questions: Why do you feel obligated? Where is it written that you are obligated? Who obligated you? What do you feel obligated to do? Be as realistic and as reasonable as possible.

☐ I think of myself as a good partner/friend/child/parent.

_____

_____

☐ They need me.

_____

_____

☐ They gave me something and I should be grateful.

_____

_____

☐ People are supposed to love their partner/friend/child/parent.

_____

_____

☐ I am trying to live up to the expectations of my partner/friend/child/parent.

_____

_____

☐ If I didn't do this, people would think badly of me.

_____

_____

☐ I put this much time into this relationship; why quit now?

_____

_____

☐ People like me have a duty.

_____

_____

☐ My religion teaches me to be this way.

_____

_____

☐ My parents taught me that I should do this.

_____

_____

☐ If I didn't live up to my obligations, I would feel like a bad person.

_____

_____

☐ My values prevent me from setting boundaries.

_____

_____

☐ They never fail to remind me what I owe them.

_____

_____

Guilt

"Emotional blackmailers encourage us to take global responsibility for their complaints and unhappiness, doing all they can to reprogram the basic and necessary mechanisms of appropriate guilt into an undeserved guilt-production line where the lights continually flash 'guilty, guilty, guilty'" (Forward and Frazier 1997, 54).

Fill in the blanks in the lines below to make the statements specific to your life. Then, on a scale of 1 to 5, rate your sense of guilt.

_____ I feel guilty for feeling _____ instead of _____.

_____ I hate _____ so much that I just say "_____" and hope that ends it.

_____ I feel like a bad person when _____.

_____ If I had known about BPD or NPD earlier, I wouldn't have _____.

_____ When they feel _____ they blame it on me.

_____ I would _____ if it weren't for the fact that I would feel guilty.

_____ They blame me for _____.

_____ Sometimes I feel guilty for thinking _____.

_____ Sometimes I feel guilty for doing _____.

_____ Sometimes I feel guilty for being _____.

_____ Sometimes I feel guilty for having _____.

_____ I did _____ years ago and I still feel guilty.

_____ I was told that I was guilty for _____.

_____ Sometimes I feel guilty for _____.

Consider these questions and reflect in the space below. Why do you feel guilty? Where is it written that you are guilty? Who served as judge and jury? How long is your sentence? Be as realistic and as reasonable as possible.

Cutting Through the FOG

In real life, fog can lead to collisions, people getting lost, and general confusion. FOG can do the same thing. FOG destroys relationships because the people who exploit it are not acting out of love or caring. Real love isn't won by manipulation. It only leads to anger, burnout, resentment, and sometimes the loss of the relationship. When you eliminate the FOG, your loved one can clearly ask for what they want and you can choose to give it because that is what they genuinely want to do.

Violinists do not wake up one day and decide to play a concerto with the New York Philharmonic. For every minute you see in performance, they may have practiced for years. Some smokers quit several times before they quit for good. Even if you've tried to combat emotional blackmail before and have been less than successful, you can still do it once you've learned and practiced the techniques.

In the following exercise, you can practice combating emotional blackmail. Like many other life changes, it's a skill that requires *inner motivation*, a *commitment to change*, *practice*, and *follow-through*.

Inner Motivation: Calculate the costs of giving in to emotional blackmail. Check off those costs that are appropriate to your situation.

- ☐ Feelings of anger, irritation, being used, trapped, stressed, burned out, manipulated, confused, resentful, hurt, frustrated, overwhelmed, unlovable, discouraged.

- ☐ Loss of self-respect, control, integrity; loss of time for yourself or time you had planned for yourself and others; loss of pleasure in the relationship; loss of possibilities to be a good role model.

- ☐ Other problems: feeling forced to agree when you disagree; being thought of as a "softy"; feeling discouraged when you try to stand up for yourself; being more concerned about what others think of you than what you think of yourself; avoiding places where you might run into the blackmailer; and not feeling in charge of your own life. Worst of all (at least in an adult relationship you've chosen) is that you are not happy with a situation *you agreed to of your own accord.*

Commitment to Change: Make a "commitment to change" certificate in your notebook. Write out a contract with yourself, spelling out your personal limits. Spell out the good things that will happen when you do. What do you want to do? Under what conditions are you willing to accommodate others? How often? Will you expect anything in return? You must make the benefits tangible so it feels like you are gaining something: reclaiming your integrity. Don't worry if you're not perfect. No one is—especially people learning a new skill.

Practice: If you have a hard time saying "no" to anyone, start with declining simple requests you don't want to do for people who do not have BPD or NPD. Just like our violinist did not start with the New York Philharmonic, don't start with your loved one. Look for other opportunities when less is at stake and the people making the request do not have a personality disorder. Take an assertiveness class. Learn to walk before you learn to run.

Forward (1997) recommends that you *do not defend or explain your decision to the blackmailer.* This may seem like a bold step—you may think, "At least I offer them an explanation." But most of the time you actually don't. Now, if you and your partner agreed to have children and you changed your mind, the situation would be different. But if you try to explain every decision you make and feel the need to justify and explain it, you may be talking apples while your loved one is talking oranges. The point is you want to change your way of life while someone else is seeing a particular request in isolation. Excuses only give them ammunition.

Let's say that they assume you will be there to pick them up after work. But let's say that they rarely ask or understand that you have to take off work or otherwise rearrange your schedule to do so, and you feel taken for granted. The more you try to explain they will have to take the bus, the more they will push your "obligation" and "guilt" buttons. If you simply but firmly say, "It's just not going to work out for me this time," instead of "I have to work," you don't give them anything to work with, such as, "What's more important, me or your job?"

Follow-through: Repeat the following phrases as often as necessary and do not fall into the trap of explaining your decision. Some people only listen to explanations to find a flaw in reasoning so that they can back you into a corner. Think of a small child asking, "Why can't I eat all my Halloween candy now?" a dozen times while you tick off twelve reasons.

- I'm sorry, I won't be able to.
- I'm sorry that makes you upset.
- I just can't do that.
- I understand you feel that way, but I'm going to have to say no.
- That's your choice. This is mine.
- I understand I've done that before, but this time I can't.
- You may have a point, but I can't do it this time.

Stop walking on eggshells.

- I understand you feel that way. I hope you find another solution.

- I see you're disappointed. I hope you find another answer to your problem.

- Threatening me isn't going to work. I've made my decision and I'm asking you to respect that.

Come up with your own phrase to use as a response to emotional blackmail.

_____

Action Step: Anticipate and Practice

In the space below, describe an entire conversation in which you are being emotionally blackmailed. What is the blackmailer likely to want? What pressure or threats will they use?

_____

_____

_____

_____

_____

_____

_____

_____

_____

_____

Now, go back to your worst-case and best-case scenarios. Remember that each person is responsible for their own actions. That means you own your decision and the blackmailer owns theirs. There is a high likelihood that you will feel uncomfortable with it at first. But each time you do this successfully, you will gain a newfound respect for yourself and become more confident. And it will be easier to do the next time.

If they notice a change in your outlook and say so, avoid saying something that could imply "I'm putting myself first, now." While that may be true, saying it would push a very hot fear-of-abandonment button. The better you can meet your own needs in this relationship, the more likely it is that the relationship will improve.

Keep the Benefits in Mind

Change will be difficult for both you and the blackmailer. So it's vital to keep in mind that you're doing this both to reclaim your life and to ensure the health of the relationship. You won't be happy in the long term in a relationship in which you feel you're being blackmailed. If it's a relationship you value, ending it or detaching yourself emotionally would probably be more painful than learning to address their blackmail in a healthy way. At the same time, you're teaching them better ways to get what they need while you take care of you. Keep telling yourself, "I *can* stand this feeling. This is what it feels like to make adult choices. This is normal."

Now that we've discussed the basics of emotional blackmail, we'll take an overall look at choosing the right words and knowing which path to take when trying to be heard by someone who has borderline or narcissistic personality disorder.

Reflection

After reading this chapter, what stands out to you?

_____

_____

_____

_____

_____

_____

_____

_____

_____

What have you learned in this chapter that you want to put into action?

_____

_____

_____

_____

_____

_____

_____

_____

_____

_____

CHAPTER 8

Being Heard: Communicating with an HCP

It's scary, telling another person "This is who I am. This is what I want." Scarier still is standing by the truth about ourselves—our integrity—as we must when we give the other person a choice to accept or not accept our decisions and differences … But remember we're asking for something that is absolutely reasonable: We want the other person to stop manipulating us.

—Susan Forward, *Emotional Blackmail*

When emotions are high, your HCP can't "hear" you. There is a reason why.

Here's what's happening: The emotional part of the brain is taking over in the same way that shock and denial help protect people who have just suffered a loss. Intellectually, they understand what's happening. But the "emotional" part of the brain is crowding out the cognitive (thinking) part. Imagine a clogged sink. The water (rational thinking) is mostly blocked by built-up hair, scum, and whatever else is in there from the past (the emotions).

This is one reason why being intelligent is a handicap for both of you. You keep expecting things to make sense. How can you be at fault for something that happened *before you met them*? How can they "win" when they're damned if they do and damned if they don't? The more time you spend searching for logical answers, the more time you will waste. And the smarter you are, the more difficult it is to understand why your loved one behaves in ways that are counterproductive.

Using DEAR with Ragers

If the HCP is a rager, choose a time of relative calm to set a limit regarding rages. Use DEAR methods at a time when your loved one is able to listen and respond. Tell them that you will not endure rages and you will only talk to them when they are able to have a meaningful conversation. Explain that if they get angry, you will simply leave the room or otherwise exit until they can have a reasonable, two-way conversation.

If during this discussion your loved one goes into a rage, leave the room and try to set the limit at another time. If they simply won't listen, leave, just as you would if someone were holding a knife and threatening to use it. Would you ask for the person's permission to get out of the way? Verbal abuse can be just as dangerous, though people tend to take it less seriously. Do not expose yourself or your children to cutting verbal remarks. Get the children to safety, just as you would if they were being physically threatened. Verbal abuse is more insidious and just as dangerous to their mental health.

If your loved one is a rager in the car, take an Uber. Take the bus. Skip the trip. Buy a unicycle. Get a ride. *Do not put yourself in the position of being trapped with them.*

After you set the limit, you must follow through with it. Telling them "If you XX, I will XX" and not following through will be the single biggest mistake you ever make in the relationship. When you don't follow through, you are saying, "Just kidding, you know I'm weak!" That acts as a reward and reinforces the behavior. When you sometimes reward someone and sometimes don't, it just teaches the person to keep doing whatever it is that they're doing (or not doing). This is a scientific principle, not something I just came up with.

If your loved one cannot control themselves around the children, take the children somewhere else. Do not allow children to be raged at or even to witness rages. If you think they might hurt the pets, gather up the animals as well. If you still feel unsafe, call 911.

Action Step: Leaving During a Rage

The following are several ways to "leave." Check the ones that you can use.

- ☐ Hang up the phone. Make sure you can't hear texts.

- ☐ Go to a different room.

- ☐ Take the laundry and go to a laundromat.

- ☐ Delete e-mail. Filter out your loved one's address.

- ☐ Take a taxi.

- ☐ Put on earbuds and rock to your favorite song.

- ☐ Take the kids to a place of their choosing.

- ☐ Visit a friend.

- ☐ Arrange ahead of time for a friend to pick you up. Call them and wait outside at a previously designated place.

- ☐ If you are afraid for your physical safety, have a bag packed ahead of time with necessary items and plan where you will go. You can find a full list of preparations at any domestic violence website. Always document any physical injuries and file a report with the police.

One Key to Being Heard

People with BPD may interpret innocent comments in ways the speaker doesn't intend, and may even think their loved one is putting them down.

Teresa Whitehurst, PhD, teaches families how to recognize BPD symptoms, predict triggers, and use verbal, nonverbal, and other forms of communication in an attempt to offer empathy and avoid triggering symptoms. She teaches them how to word their sentences carefully to help diffuse potentially explosive situations. "To people who are diagnosed with BPD, words make a huge difference in how they feel about themselves, others, and the future," Whitehurst told me in an interview. "Family members who learn to accurately translate their loved one's 'language' more than 50 percent of the time heighten their sense of safety, of being okay, and of being heard and understood."

Whitehurst recommends that family members watch for small signs and subtle mood shifts that can warn them of pending rages or acting out *before* they happen. "Translation is only the first step of the process, however," she says. "You need the right words to respond to mood shifts, angry accusations, or acting-out behaviors with empathy instead of anger."

Whitehurst has found that certain phrases more than others help people with BPD feel that their family members are sensitive to their feelings and needs. In my experience, most people with a loved one with BPD feel that things should be the other way around—that people with BPD should be more sensitive to *them*. This may be true. But BPD can prevent people from validating you, just like a damaged spinal cord can prevent people from walking. If you look at the situation this way—that you are helping them do something they don't have the tools to do—you can feel better about the extra effort it takes to learn these communication skills.

Whitehurst says, "Attuning ourselves to people with BPD with accurate translation and empathetic responses serves to encourage them to use the highest level of communication—verbal communication—and can calm the agitated (and sometimes crisis-provoking) emotions and fears common to BPD."

Practice, Practice, Practice

Whitehurst recommends practicing certain phrases with friends and other family members before you attempt to use them in a heated situation with your loved one. These phrases appear in the following exercise.

Action Step: Memorize These Phrases

Complete the following phrases by filling in the blanks. Pick your favorites to write down on notecards or in your phone. Carry them with you, and memorize them while you are standing in line, waiting, or have a free minute or two.

1. "To me, it sounds like you may be feeling a little _____."

2. "I'm hearing _____. Are you feeling _____

   because of _____?"

3. "I'm wondering if something I've said or done might have contributed to your feeling [irritable/

   angry/anxious] _____."

4. "I may be wrong about this, but I'm wondering if you're feeling kind of [lonely/let down/betrayed/

   discouraged] _____?"

5. "If this had happened to me, I would be feeling _____. How about you?"

6. "I feel _____ when you begin to _____."

7. Can we continue this discussion in about _____ [minutes/hours]?"

Using "I" Statements

All of the sentences in the preceding exercise have two things in common:

1. They center the word "I." You're the world's leading expert on your own feelings. No one can take them away, dub them "justified" or "unjustified," or change them, although you can change them yourself. If your loved one does say, "You shouldn't feel that way," simply say, "But I do. Feelings don't always make sense and they don't have to. Feelings just are. I respect yours and I hope you can respect mine."

2. The statements don't presume to know how your loved one feels. Even if they are raging louder than a car alarm at 1 a.m., they may deny or be unaware of their anger. They may be sobbing like Niagara Falls, yet deny that they're sad. And perhaps they're tears of joy. Being concerned without assuming what's on their mind or at their emotional center can lead to better communication.

"By using responses such as these more or less consistently over time, you can eventually transform your loved one's relationship with you," Whitehurst explains. "If the person with BPD is in therapy, this modification can provide a powerful boost to your loved one's efforts to grow in emotional self-control, maturity, and self-esteem."

What to Remember

- Remember that phrases, however brilliantly they're used, can't cure BPD or NPD. Additionally, phrases may work some of the time but not all of the time. This doesn't mean you've failed. It simply means that every situation is different.

- Don't chastise yourself for forgetting these phrases and accept that this new language will not be appropriate every time. No change works overnight, and you've been communicating in other ways for months or years. Just like there's no diet pill that keeps the fat off painlessly and permanently, communication techniques are not cures but *tools* that can help when used correctly in the right circumstances with the right person in the best frame of mind.

- When your loved one suddenly becomes depressed, angry, or argumentative, it's easy to fall into old, quarrelsome patterns. Writing down or, better yet, memorizing a variety of responses for different situations can get both of you onto a more positive path when you find yourself faced with an unexpected quarrel or emotional state.

Different Responses for Different Moods

HCPs—children especially—can easily change the mood of an entire household within thirty seconds. By changing your responses from combative to collaborative, you may be able to avert an argument or temper tantrum. The following are some of Whitehurst's suggested responses for different moods. This table expands on the previous list and indicates appropriate versus inappropriate responses to different situations.

Situation	Invalidating Responses	Wise Responses
Family member's mood seems to be sinking, *although they haven't said so.*	Cheer up. Do you want to see a movie? What's the problem?	I may be wrong, but you seem a little down. How are you feeling? It might help to talk about how you're feeling. When would you like to talk? I'm wondering what would help you right now?
They tell you that they are feeling anxious, sad, irritable, or depressed.	What is it *now*? Don't be sad. Don't take it out on me. Don't worry.	Do you want to talk about it? Is there some way I can help? It's great you're telling me how you feel in words; this helps me understand you better.

Situation	Invalidating Responses	Wise Responses
They are showing you their feelings by acting out: crying, screaming, slamming doors, throwing things, cursing, the silent treatment.	Stop it, leave me alone. Control yourself, act like an adult. Are you mad at me? You're acting spoiled. Please talk to me. I'm so worried about you. As long as you're living under my roof, you'll do what I say! Get out of my face.	I can see how upset you are and I'd like to talk with you about the situation if you calm down a bit. I love you and I want to hear what's going on in your mind and heart. But I can't help you until you can sit down and talk to me. What would help you calm down right now? I can't hear your complaints against me until I feel safe. If you're feeling extremely angry or out of control, let's take a break and then meet to talk about it later. I promise to listen.

Responding to Incorrect Assumptions

HCPs are often so caught up in their own emotions they make false assumptions about what you do and say. If they don't understand your reasoning, try one or more of the following sample responses from Whitehurst:

- "If I've said or done anything to cause you distress, I hope you'll tell me."

- "Sounds like when I said that, you started to feel sad/anxious/stressed/annoyed/distracted."

- "No wonder you're feeling angry/worried/disappointed/confused."

- "I hope you'll believe me when I say I didn't *intend* any harm when I said/did that, yet it sounds like my statement/action nonetheless did cause you distress/difficulty."

- "I hope that you can forgive me. I also hope you hear me when I say that I didn't *intend* this result/problem/feeling for you."

- "I'm wondering if we can think of ways to prevent this kind of problem in the future; do you have some ideas?"

Snippy Remarks and Sarcasm

Snippy or sarcastic comments are difficult to respond to because they're often vague, indirect, and meant to hurt (not to communicate). It's the verbal equivalent of a schoolyard bully taunting someone to "push me," to give them an excuse to smack you in the face. So the best way to handle these kinds of statements is to minimize them, purposely misunderstand their intent, and avoid giving them the importance that your loved one would like them to have.

Responding to Sarcasm

Don't JADE—justify, argue, defend, or explain. This just results in chaos. You don't justify because they are in their own world. Arguing embroils you in an argument—or causes you to withdraw, which implies you will let yourself be verbally abused. Instead, do one or more of the following:

- Pretend ignorance of malicious intent. If your loved one says, "Boy, that chocolate cake sure has a lot of calories," implying you shouldn't eat it, you might say, "I know; isn't it great?"

- Recognize that your critic has an opinion, even if you don't agree. If they say, "I can't believe you'd do that!" you might say, "It's true that you wouldn't do it." If your teen says, "I can't believe you won't let me go to Aaron's party, just because his parents are away. I hate you!" you might say, "I know it seems to you as if we're the meanest parents on the planet, but that's the way it is."

- If your loved one says something sarcastic or makes negative comments about an opinion you've expressed, make a noncommittal, vague statement, such as, "Some people think that way," or "Whatever you say." Say it in a carefree way that shows you don't particularly care about their opinion. Rephrasing someone else's inane or careless remark as a question often just shows how illogical it is. If they say, "You can't go to the park because it's 2 p.m. and we eat dinner at 6 p.m.," respond with, "So you're saying we can't go to the park now at 2 p.m. because we're eating dinner at 6 p.m.?"

Here are the three most important points to remember:

1. Don't let a hurtful comment go unacknowledged, even if your response is to get up and walk away, saying you have important things to do. Over time, little drops of venom build up and become very toxic to your mental health.

2. Don't show you take the comments seriously by arguing or doing what they are doing.

3. DO NOT JADE: justify, argue, defend yourself, or explain.

Action Step: Practice, Practice, and Practice Some More

New ways of reacting do not come automatically. You need to work on change for it to be effective.

1. Think back and write your loved one's typical sarcastic comments below.

    _____

    _____

    _____

    _____

    _____

2. Using possible responses given in this chapter as a guideline, write down the answers that feel most comfortable for you.

    _____

    _____

    _____

    _____

    _____

    _____

3. When you are alone, practice saying each of these phrases out loud. Keep saying them until you feel the words rolling smoothly off your tongue.

4. Write down an imagined response from your loved one.

_____

_____

_____

5. Practice repeating the same phrase (the "broken record" technique). Envision yourself remaining calm and in control. Take deep breaths and visualize yourself repeating the comments until you can do so without your heart beating faster or until your sense of discomfort fades. No matter what they say, simply repeat your response. Pretend they are dangling a fishhook at you, daring you to bite and be dragged into an argument. You simply have to refuse to take the bait.

6. Go to a good friend, explain what you are doing, and ask the friend to play the part of your family member. Practice until you feel comfortable. Make sure you feel comfortable with all possible responses, from raging to the silent treatment. If you don't know someone you can ask to play their role, record the comments you imagine they will make. Then you can practice responding, using the recording you've made.

Having Your Point of View Acknowledged

At some point, many HCPs are able to have an actual discussion without raging or being biting. At these times, they are the most open to your point of view. But it's a two-way street, and you will probably have to show good faith first by indicating that you are listening to what they are saying. This kind of conversation takes the most skill.

The following is a simple three-step technique you can use during the entire conversation. It requires _repeating_ what they say, _responding_ to it with feeling and using "I" statements, and _acknowledging_ you may have two different opinions.

Step 1: Repeating

Repeat (quote or paraphrase) your loved one's point while making eye contact. This does not mean you are agreeing with them. You are simply showing that you have heard them. _When people feel heard, they feel better, even if the other person hasn't agreed with them._

You need to work on listening to them, rather than waiting for your turn to talk. Simply listen and understand the point(s) well enough to repeat them. If you need to, ask them to slow down. After you have repeated what they said, ask "Is this what you meant to say?" If not, ask them to repeat it.

At first, simply repeat what your family member says. After you feel comfortable with this, try to include a "feeling phrase," asking them if they are feeling a certain way.

Action Step: Repeating Phrases

When you repeat what they said, it is important that you don't sound condescending, angry, or patronizing. You also don't want to sound like you're simply parroting phrases. Try to achieve a tone that says, "I'm listening closely to what you're saying." Fill in the following helpful phrases using words that paraphrase comments your HCP has made. Use your notebook if you need more room.

- So what you're saying is you believe that _____?

- You seem to think that _____ . Is this right?

- So, if I have this right, you want _____?

- Let me make sure I am hearing you. You want me to _____?

- You say you believe that _____ . Is that what you meant to say?

- It sounds like you're feeling _____ . Am I right?

Now, practice these phrases until you memorize them and can say them aloud with the right tone of voice. Practice by saying them to a friend who is willing to play the role of your loved one.

Step 2: Responding

In a perfect world, you would respond to their comments and they would confirm that they understand you by repeating what *you* said. But this is probably not possible because it requires skills your loved one may not have. However, you can validate yourself simply by making your own statement and reassuring yourself that you, like them, have a right to your point of view, opinions, and reactions. I strongly recommend that even if you have a therapist, you surround yourself with a group of friends who will listen to you vent. If you are lucky, one of them will be especially witty and will have you laughing instead of crying in sadness or frustration.

Many years ago, I was faced with a serious situation involving a custody dispute between someone with BPD and their former partner. I used to get together with a friend who was equally angry about the situation and we would make up songs that the person with BPD would never hear. Even though I knew all about the person's pain and why they were doing what they did, it didn't make me feel any better. So we would make up songs about them, using familiar melodies and changing the words. We would take turns, competing to see who could come up with the most outrageous lyrics. During a three-hour car trip, we must have exhausted every tune I know. Today, I still remember the fun of singing those songs. And since no one heard the songs but us, no one was hurt. You need to vent your frustration.

An "I" statement is one that cannot be argued with. If a child says, "My little brother acts like a monster," you can respond with your own opinion of the little brother's behavior. But if the child says, "I am jealous of my little brother," you cannot tell her she doesn't feel that way. She does feel that way. You can try to help her feel less jealous by spending more time with her, but you cannot (and should not) tell her what to feel. *Feelings are not right or wrong, justified or unjustified. They just are.* Make sure your feeling statement is *not* an opinion, such as "I feel you are wrong." A feeling is one word, some variation on mad, sad, glad, scared, or confused. You can follow up the feeling statement with another "I" statement that describes your opinion or point of view.

Rather than argue with their reality, simply put yours next to theirs. You truth is just as valid. For example, if your family member says, "I hate bees," you would *not* say, "You should like bees because they play an important role in pollination." You might say, "I appreciate bees. Without them, plants might not get pollinated." It may be a subtle difference, but you don't need to contradict or invalidate their views or feelings to present your own.

Feeling and "I" Statements

What follows are some examples of feeling statements and "I" statements. You can fill in the blanks with words appropriate to your own circumstance.

- "I don't feel that way. I feel _____."

- "I feel misunderstood. My intention was to _____."

- "I am confused about _____. What do you mean?"

- "I feel differently about that. My opinion is _____."

- "I am sorry you believe that I meant to hurt you. When I said _____

  my intention was to _____."

- "I love _____ and would never purposely do anything to_____."

Step 3: Acknowledging

Rather than argue your position, simply acknowledge that you both have the right to your own feelings and opinions about whatever the subject is. Sample phrases include:

- I guess we can agree to disagree.

- Let's say we both have our own opinions and leave it at that.

- I understand. You feel that . . . and I believe that . . . There are always at least two ways to look at something.

Reflection

After reading this chapter, what stands out to you?

_____

_____

_____

_____

_____

_____

_____

_____

What have you learned in this chapter that you want to put into action?

_____

_____

_____

_____

_____

_____

_____

_____

CHAPTER 9

Diagnosing the Relationship

This chapter will discuss both intimate partner relationships and parent-child relationships. First, let's look closely at skills to support you if your partner is an HCP.

When the HCP Is Your Partner

Start by answering the following questions:

- When you think about the times when things were best, had you settled into a period of real intimacy and knowledge about your partner? Or were you still in the putting-on-your-best-face early stages of the relationship? In other words, are you longing for the person your partner actually was, or the person they were pretending to be?

_____

_____

_____

_____

_____

- How important are the needs that they cannot fulfill, and how long are you willing to wait to see if your partner will try to fulfill your other needs?

_____

_____

_____

_____

_____

- Has there been more than one instance of physical violence toward you or any children? If so, I advise you to seriously consider leaving, and if you haven't done so, make sure you put together a safety plan (appendix C).

  _____

  _____

  _____

  _____

  _____

- Flip a coin. Heads, you stay, tails, you leave. Before you flip the coin, stop and close your eyes. Pretend it's heads. How do you feel? Pretend it's tails. How do you feel? When the coin lands, you may find your true feelings emerging.

  _____

  _____

  _____

  _____

- Does your partner seem to deliberately avoid giving you what you need— even the smallest little thing? If so, they may have an above-average need for power and control. This gets old very fast and is an intimacy destroyer.

  _____

  _____

  _____

  _____

  _____

- Has the situation progressed to the point where you feel invisible or humiliated most of the time? Does your partner shut you up when you want to talk about things that are important to you? Is your self-esteem so tiny you couldn't find it even with a police sniffing dog? You don't need a counselor to tell you this relationship is toxic to your self-esteem.

_____

_____

_____

_____

_____

- Is your partner a habitual liar? Would they rather lie than tell the truth? Is this such a problem you've become cynical?

_____

_____

_____

_____

_____

- When you think about all that you've given in this relationship, do you suppose it's realistic to expect the score will ever be evened up? If not, does this bother you?

_____

_____

_____

_____

_____

- Does your partner take any responsibility for the problems in the relationship? Have they told you this won't change? After many years of studying BPD, I have found that willingness to look at problems *together* is a better predictor of long-term success than any other factor.

_____

_____

_____

_____

- Have you fallen into the "waiting trap?" The trap works like this: Say you push the "up" button for the elevator. You wait. One minute. Two. Three. Soon you realize that you only need to go up two flights and the stairs are right there. But now it's been four minutes. You're sure the elevator will come about the same time you open the door to the stairs. Besides, you've already waited five—no, six minutes. At seven minutes, the elevator arrives. It takes another minute to load and unload everyone. Congratulations. You've fallen into the waiting trap. A five-minute trip has taken ten. The marriage waiting trap works much like this. If you've been waiting five years for your partner to change, what's another year or two or three? But three years becomes thirty and nothing has changed. Set a date for when you expect "things to get better" and make a decision with no more waiting.

_____

_____

_____

_____

Give yourself a reasonable date for your partner to make the changes you've requested. If they haven't made them by then, there's a good chance they never will. Remember that actions speak louder than words.

- Are you limiting even the good times with your partner for fear they will turn into bad times; for example, do you avoid sharing thoughts or feelings, asking questions, inviting them to outings, discussing questions, and sharing good or bad moments in your day? Do the good times scare you because you know the bad times can't be far behind?

_____

_____

_____

_____

- Can you articulate what you would miss about your partner? Are they generic things like "company" and "shared expenses" instead of personal things like "their great sense of humor?"

_____

_____

_____

_____

- Does your partner "fight dirty?" Are you afraid to try to negotiate because they have more weapons and are more willing to use them against you? Does it seem that your partner is more for themself than for the partnership?

_____

_____

_____

_____

The Security Factor

People who value the security of being in a relationship more than the relationship itself may:

- Feel weak and helpless

- Wait for their partner to leave first

- Feel that there is no way out

- Feel they can't live without their spouse

- Feel afraid of the future and paralyzed

- Feel afraid of the disapproval of others

- Use excuses and dodges to stay in their partnership (e.g., "I'm the only one who can make them happy")

- Have decided to get out before, but backed down at their loved one's use of fear, obligation, and guilt

Staying in a relationship with your partner for security is pointless. High-conflict people are emotionally unstable, and looking to them for stability is hopeless. Think about what you're already providing for yourself in this relationship. What exactly is it that you would be giving up? And is there another way to get it? Write your answers in the blank space provided here.

_____

_____

_____

_____

_____

_____

Action Step: Avoiding Making a Decision

Someone once said, "Not to decide is to decide." Sometimes not making a decision about your situation is, in fact, making a decision. The following are reasons that some people give for waiting and waiting. If any of them feel familiar, check them off, and write down your thoughts in your notebook.

☐ **"Hey, I've got kids!"** Lots of people do. Yet this hasn't stopped them from going after what they want. While things have become more enlightened in recent years, it's true that in some courtrooms, custody laws and tradition favor the mother assuming custody. Some men use this fact as an excuse to avoid making a tough choice. They complain they won't get custody or joint custody even though:

They have no idea what the laws are in their state or how the process goes. Rather than read a book, they rely on hearsay and believe the worst-case scenarios.

They have never seen a lawyer, or they have been scared off by one pessimistic lawyer.

They have never spoken to anyone from a fathers' or children's rights organization to learn how to obtain what they want.

They let themselves believe that the effect of divorce on children is worse than the effect of living in an abusive environment.

_____

_____

_____

_____

_____

_____

_____

☐ **"I'm waiting for my partner to get better."** If your partner is in therapy and the two of you are both finding new ways to communicate, this makes sense. But if your partner is in denial, seeing a therapist only to please you or to keep the status quo, or they are actively making your life miserable, you have not yet accepted the fact that this is as good as it gets. Is this good enough? Good enough for the rest of your life? Good enough for your children?

_____

_____

_____

_____

_____

_____

☐ **"I don't want to be alone!"** This is a very common fear perpetuated in part by our society, where twosomes rule. If this is your fear, ask yourself how much company and friendship you're getting from your partner *now*. Take stock of your friends and family and take note of who will support you if you decide to leave. Write down in your journal what you will *gain* from being alone: no more rages, criticisms, blaming, or trying to please someone who won't be pleased, etc. You took care of your emotional needs for years before you met this person. You can do it again. Make a list of the things you would enjoy more if the HCP were not in your life.

_____

_____

_____

_____

_____

☐ **"I wouldn't leave if they had cancer. Why would I leave if they have BPD or NPD?"** This analogy is *not* accurate. If your partner had cancer, they would be getting treatment. Many unconventional types don't. Someone with cancer doesn't manage their feelings by continually taking them out on others. Someone with BPD or NPD may. Partners work together to fight cancer and support each other. Loved ones of HCPs have all the blame

Stop Walking on Eggshells Workbook, 2nd Edition

laid on them and are treated *like* a cancer. If your HCP is working on treatment, then the analogy makes more sense. If they're not, it doesn't.

_____

_____

_____

_____

_____

_____

_____

☐ **"No one else would want me."** This is a sure sign you need to leave this relationship now.

_____

_____

_____

_____

_____

_____

_____

_____

What About Therapy?

Many people try individual or couples therapy.

If your partner is convinced that everyone else has a problem—not them—beware. The combination of this and a bad therapist can be deadly. If your partner can fool people, you may be terribly invalidated.

Trust your intuition. This applies to both couples and individual counseling. Does the clinician seem to *get it*? Have years gone by without real progress? Does your partner seem to be using therapy as a false move toward progress? Have either of you gained any insight? (Your children, if you have them, might need therapy as well; there is much information about children and therapy online.)

I am sorry to say this, but I have never heard from anyone that couples therapy worked. Your partner is just too well-defended. You know they think everything is your fault, and their sole reason for being there is to convince the therapist to agree. Couples therapy requires that both people are reasonable and participate equally. If the therapist is a good one, they will ferret out the truth, and your partner will quit therapy because they feel that either the therapist favors you or they are incompetent.

However, therapy is a great idea for YOU. It can get you unstuck, help you recognize toxic patterns, and validate you. There is a subconscious reason why you chose your partner and they chose you, and that you've stayed so long with a toxic partner when other people would have left.

The best clinicians strike a balance between exploring the past (childhood, relationships with parents, etc.) and modifying behaviors that must change *now*. For example, if you overeat in response to your situation, you can work on finding a different coping strategy even as you explore your situation on a deeper level. If your partner rages, the clinician can help you set boundaries even before the disorder itself is addressed.

If You Decide to Leave

If you leave the relationship, there is a very good chance that your partner's abandonment fears will kick in and they will try to pull you back into the relationship by any means possible. This ranges from promises of change and declarations of love to threats: "You'll never see the children again!" This behavior pattern is so common that online support group members have named it "hoovering" because it feels like you're getting "sucked" back in by a vacuum cleaner.

Being "hoovered" is a bit like hungrily biting into a sandwich, only to find it's made out of plastic. But most people are so eager for their partner to change they willingly eat the plastic and pretend it's duck à l'orange from a fancy French restaurant. If you don't watch out, you and your partner will be caught in an endless loop of forgiveness, a buildup of blame and criticism, you threatening to leave and being hoovered back into the relationship. Some people spend years in this cycle.

Action Step: Turn Off That Hoover

Here are some ideas for combating being hoovered, or being sucked back into the relationship. Check off the ideas that appeal to you and use your notebook to plan what you will do when you've left the relationship but your partner is trying to get you back.

☐ Journal, journal, journal. Start right now and document everything you can remember that ever really hurt you in the course of the relationship: phrases used to malign you, irrational arguments, infidelities, embarrassing rages in public, pathological jealousies, verbal, physical, and emotional abuse.

☐ After each failed attempt to "make your opinion known" that is met with anger and rejection by your partner, write down your point of view. Then imagine what it would be like to be with a partner who could really hear it and respect it.

☐ Hang out with "normal" people (using "normal" very loosely): good friends, family (if this applies), colleagues, and anyone with whom you can have good, deep, honest conversations. Then contrast any of those conversations to your most recent attempt at an in-depth conversation with your partner.

☐ Go through your photo collection and look at pictures of you. Look at how happy you looked! How long has it been since you looked that happy? How long since you've had a really good night's sleep or woken up with a spring in your step and a smile on your face that wasn't "bought" at the cost of some emotional compromise?

☐ Make a list of things that bother you about your partner that might not even have anything to do with their BPD traits.

☐ Buy some books about codependency and addictive relationships. Read them religiously. Fill in the goofy self-help questionnaires. Highlight passages. Do some serious and honest thinking about your own past and what emotional patterns in yourself might be compelling you back into this kind of unfulfilling, non-reciprocal relationship.

Like many Action Steps, this one involves changing your thinking, evaluating your values, and questioning your assumptions. Getting rid of the sticky cobwebs in your head takes time, effort, and the right tools. Before you go back to this relationship, wait for your partner to enter therapy and learn to treat you in the way you want to be treated. Not falling for their "take me back" techniques may be the motivation they need to do just that.

When the HCP Is Your Child

If you're the parent of an HCP, there is good news and bad news. The good news is that treatment works! The bad news is that:

- They must want therapy for themselves.

- They must work hard in therapy. The more effort your child puts in, the more they will get out of treatment, and the fuller their recovery will be.

- It generally takes six to twelve months for better behavior and managed emotions to take effect.

But when the person with BPD or NPD truly commits to recovery, the right treatment can help reduce the frequency and intensity of their symptoms, and perhaps eliminate some traits altogether.

BPD and NPD are like chronic physical illnesses for which a person might need to deal with persistent symptoms. For example, for a person in recovery from BPD, the tendency to fear abandonment is still there, but it doesn't necessarily lead to impulsive, reckless behavior. Through treatment, they learn to recognize when they are operating from their fear of being abandoned. For example, a friend who doesn't smile at them in the hallway vs. a friend who says they don't want to be friends anymore.

The most prevalent standardized therapy designed for BPD is dialectical behavior therapy. DBT is the brainchild of Marsha S. Linehan, a psychologist who recovered from BPD herself. Fundamental DBT concepts include:

Patients must be motivated and willing to change. If your child doesn't meet this criterion, it may be best to hold off on DBT because it is expensive and a lot of work, with therapy twice a week and homework in between. Each child is assigned to a therapist, who directs the conversation, and a group skills-training session. DBT has four key skill modules: core mindfulness, distress tolerance, emotional regulation, and interpersonal relationships (Linehan 2015).

Core mindfulness: Mindfulness is being present in the now, paying attention to the environment, thoughts, and feelings. Mindfulness is beneficial for every family member.

Distress tolerance: This is being able to sit with painful feelings without making things worse.

Emotional regulation: This is managing negative and overwhelming emotions while increasing positive ones. This module has three components: understanding your emotions, reducing emotional vulnerability, and changing emotional responses.

Interpersonal relationships: This means getting along better with people. The goal here is to decrease interpersonal chaos, reduce the fear of abandonment, and encourage a positive outlook.

Search online for a DBT therapist in your state or region. Barring that, New Harbinger Publications (the publisher of this and all my *Stop Walking on Eggshells* books) has many books that feature DBT skills.

The Relationship with the Therapist

The quality of the relationship between therapist and client can be more important than the type of therapy used. Some have even called it the most important common factor in successful outcomes. An American Psychological Association task force found that the relationship between a client and a therapist can be just as important as the treatment method in determining the client's success (Norcross and Wampold 2011). It is critical that the therapist make your child feel respected, validated, and understood while consistently practicing boundaries such as not engaging in self-harm behaviors during a session (yes, that has happened).

Be aware that therapists who don't specialize in treating personality disorders may not be effective at working with BPD or NPD, and in some cases, they may make it worse. For this reason, we recommend that two providers be engaged in a team approach with your child, including an experienced psychologist, therapist, or social worker, and, if medication may be needed, a psychiatrist.

The Pros and Cons of Telling Your Child About Their BPD Diagnosis

You're going to have to decide for yourself whether or not you should tell your child about their BPD diagnosis. You know your child best. Whether or not you tell your child, I don't recommend making it commonly known among friends, acquaintances, and extended family because there is so much misunderstanding and stigma surrounding the disorder. Fictional characters in books and on TV and film who are portrayed as having BPD are often not very realistic.

However, you do need support! If you have a very close relative or friend who will not judge you, will be supportive, and is willing to listen to you talk about the intricacies of the disorder, feel free to make them part of your support team. If you decide not to tell your child their diagnosis, you can explain how BPD affects them without using the term.

Pros of Disclosure

It can be a relief to the person with BPD: One of the best reasons for letting a child know about their diagnosis is to avoid them finding out on their own. Also, knowing about their diagnosis can reassure them that what they have is a known entity, that other people have it, that they can get support from these people, and, most of all, that there is treatment. Disclosure can also lead to companionship and learning: A great number of websites, self-help books, memoirs, blogs, documentaries, and YouTube videos exist about BPD, many from the point of view of the person with BPD. In addition, you won't lie by omission: At some point, perhaps in adulthood, your child may learn they have BPD. Like many people who have discovered this from a new therapist, from their case file, from an insurance company, or by accident, they may ask you why you never told them.

Cons of Disclosure

Before you tell your child, do an online search for BPD, because your child certainly will. There is a lot of depressing and stigmatizing information out there. Children can use BPD as an excuse not to take responsibility at home, school, or work.

Have a conversation with your child. You might say something like:

"I wonder if it would be helpful if you had someone to talk to besides me?"

"You appear so unhappy and sad sometimes. It breaks my heart. Maybe talking to someone will help you feel better." Point out that if they don't like the therapist or the type of therapy, they can try someone else.

"Lots of people go to therapy, even celebrities and athletes. It doesn't mean that something is wrong with them. It only means you need someone who will be there for you and only you to help you figure things out."

If you're trying to convince an adult child, you might try:

"I have a few limits if you want to live here. One of them is that you find a good therapist and work hard in therapy." Of course, you will have other boundaries. Actions speak louder than words, so you could also take the lead and go to counseling yourself. Having a child with BPD can be traumatic. Another option is family counseling, where there is no designated "problem person." Be willing to admit to your contributions to any problems.

Create a contract with your child stating that they will go to a specific number of sessions, say six, but they have to participate wholeheartedly. After that, it's their decision whether to continue.

Consider online counseling. Help them pick someone out.

Put therapy as a must-do to get certain rewards. This is not the best strategy since they need to work in therapy, but if getting them there is a matter of overcoming the unknown or fears that can dissipate, this can be a productive method.

Residential Treatment Centers

Residential treatment centers (RTCs) offer longer-term placement for children with behavioral or emotional problems that parents cannot manage at home, and other methods have not worked. Here are some examples of when an RTC might make sense:

- The child is not safe at home, perhaps because they are self-destructive.

- The family is not safe at home with the child, perhaps because they are acting out.

- You can't provide an environment that is safe and supportive of the therapeutic work, including being unable to set and maintain boundaries.

RTCs offer care 24/7 with counseling, therapy, and trained staff that may include psychiatrists, psychologists, nurses, social workers, and mental health counselors. Keep in mind that not all RTCs specialize in personality disorders and may serve children with a wide variety of issues.

Pros and Cons of Residential Treatment

Many parents who have used residential treatment will tell you that there are pros to this form of full-time treatment. One pro is that experts will be watching your child and keeping them safe. Another is that if your child can tolerate the therapy, when they leave the facility they will be more capable of leading a healthier life.

There are also cons to RTCs. Some parents regret sending their children to residential treatment because they lose control of the child's therapy. Some parents report that counselors didn't understand BPD or NPD and used therapies that are often not effective, such as complicated reward-punishment point systems. One parent said the RTC population they used mainly consisted of people with drug addictions who talked to her daughter about the pleasures of getting high.

As with choosing the right therapist, or whether or not medication is appropriate for your child, you will need to evaluate an RTC before sending your child there. Here are some things to consider (American Academy of Child and Adolescent Psychiatry 2016):

- If possible, find an RTC close to your home or near enough that you can visit your child regularly.

- Learn what you can about an RTC online. Parents in support groups may have had experience with a facility you're looking at, and they may share insights with you.

- Ask RTC staff whether they treat children with BPD symptoms. If they mainly treat children with substance abuse problems, your child may learn unwanted behaviors.

- Ask staff if they provide individual and group therapy. Their answer should be yes.

- Learn whether the facility provides academics as well as therapy, so children don't fall behind in school. If they do, are the teachers certified by the state?

- Ask if the facility is accredited. Then check with the accrediting agency to verify that the accreditation is current.

- If your child is willing to participate in their treatment, ask to do an on-site visit or tour of the facility. Try to determine how much freedom residents are allowed.

- Know that lock-down facilities are for involuntary admission, or patients who don't want to be there. A lock-down facility may be safer for children who are self-harming.

- Get all promises and policies in writing.

- Ask about the credentials of the staff and whether the facility performs background checks before hiring.

- Ask the director what provisions they have for emergency care, such as if a child gets sick or breaks an ankle.

- Ask the director how they define success with a child.

- Ask how staff handles discipline.

- Ask about their visitation policy and if children are allowed to call home.

- Ask about costs, and check with your insurance company about coverage.

Clinician's Corner with Daniel Lobel,
coauthor of *Stop Walking on Eggshell for Parents*

Your child may not want to go to residential treatment, which may cause short-term conflict because they may feel betrayed or abandoned. In the long term, though, if the treatment is successful, your child will realize that you were acting in their best interest. In fact, the choice to keep them at home would have been worse parenting. To minimize the traumatic aspects of transitioning to residential treatment, your child should know as far in advance as possible that you're considering an RTC. You may want to suggest it as a possibility as soon as possible, but not in a threatening way. Frame it as an option that's in their best interest if treatment at home is not successful.

Inpatient Hospitalization

Hospitalization may be necessary as a last resort in serious cases. The goals of inpatient hospitalization are not to treat your child or to cause lasting change. The goals are to keep your child and family safe when your child is at risk for suicide, and to stabilize the child, so they are no longer in imminent harm. During your child's stay, they will go to group sessions with people who have a variety of mental health issues. In the sessions they will learn skills to help them manage their mental health or to improve their mood. A staff psychiatrist will probably see them every day. Staff will monitor them closely for suicidal feelings, depression, anxiety, and other mental health concerns to see if they are getting better, worsening, or staying the same. Individual psychotherapy sessions are generally not helpful in an inpatient setting because the focus is keeping the patient safe, not exploring the details of their disorder. However, patients are often referred to a therapist upon discharge.

When should you consider hospitalization? When your child's suicidal thinking becomes chronic or when it becomes a suicidal plan the child intends to carry out, or when self-harm has been severe enough to require medical attention—especially if the child is also experiencing an episode of major depression or if a substance abuse problem gets worse.

If Your Teen Refuses Treatment

Every state has an age of consent, usually between fourteen and sixteen, when a child can choose whether or not to be hospitalized. If a child over that age absolutely refuses to enter a hospital or treatment facility, parents have to go the involuntary commitment route. This is not easy. The child must be an immediate danger to themselves or others, which can be difficult to prove. And it's emotionally traumatic for children and parents alike.

When the HCP Is Your Parent

This is by far the most complex relationship and one that deserves a workbook of its own. More than with any other relationship, your parent made you who you are today; made impressions when you were a small child and had no frame of reference. Therefore, rather than try to summarize a great deal of information, I will point you in the right direction to help you decide if you want to see your HCP parent, if you want to forgive them, and how to stand on your own two feet as an adult and assert yourself.

Three books I recommend are:

- *Understanding the Borderline Mother: Helping Her Children Transcend the Intense, Unpredictable, and Volatile Relationship*, by Christine Ann Lawson (2000), especially the second half.

- *Toxic Parents: Overcoming Their Hurtful Legacy and Reclaiming Your Life*, by Susan Forward (1989), especially the checklists on how you behave with your parent, how you feel when you are with them, and your beliefs about the relationship.

- *Surviving a Borderline Parent*: *How to Heal Your Childhood Wounds* and *Build Trust, Boundaries, and Self Esteem*, by Kim Roth (2004).

Read these books slowly and thoroughly, jotting down revelations in your notebook as you read them. They will take you gently through the process of learning to love yourself, despite the fact that you didn't get what you needed and you weren't adequately protected by your other parent.

Action Step: Coping with Your Emotions

This Action Step is designed to help you with your feelings about making a decision, whatever type of relationship you have. It addresses fear of the unknown—a problem we all have.

Part 1: Choose a quiet place where you will be free of distractions for about five minutes or so. Take a deep breath, relax, and free your mind of distracting thoughts. Once you're at ease, think of your greatest fear related to your loved one. What is it that they might do to help create the very worst day of your life? Picture the whole scenario, in detail, in your mind's eye. Notice the feelings it brings. Notice any sounds, sights, or even smells that come up in the mental picture. Hold that picture for a few minutes.

Once you have clearly constructed and fixed that picture in your mind, bring yourself back into the here and now. Yawn and stretch if that helps.

Part 2: Now is the time to put your thinking hat back on. In words, describe below the mental picture you just created. Realistically, what parts of the imaginary scene that you just created are really likely to occur? Make a list of these elements.

_____

_____

_____

_____

Below this list, make another list of the things that probably won't happen.

_____

_____

_____

_____

Looking at both lists, which events seem to have been created purely out of fear rather than from experience? Write them down.

_____

_____

_____

_____

_____

Now you should have three lists: the realistic events, the unrealistic events, and the events that originate from your fears. Compare and contrast the three lists.

Sometimes the logical side of our brain does not work in close harmony with the imaginative side. That can happen, for instance, if we do not acknowledge our fears. As a consequence, our fears can become like childhood monsters in the closet—never seen, but always growing in size and ferocity.

If you take the time to deliberately view something from both the logical *and* the imaginative side of your brain, then you put those two sides of yourself in dialogue with each other and they have a better opportunity to "work things out." In other words, the logical side of your brain has a better chance of filtering out the frightening "boogy men" fears.

Making Decisions to Act Differently

As human beings, we are creatures of habit. We get comfortable in our ruts, whatever they are, because adapting to our environment is a built-in survival mechanism. However, there are times and places when being comfortable with our habits and our circumstances can work against us.

In those situations, we can become habituated to things that have destructive effects on us. Whenever that happens, we can get into a condition that has been called "learned helplessness." This simply means that, consciously or unconsciously, we somehow recognize our situation as being one in which our chances of survival are better if we just lie low and don't do anything to draw attention to ourselves. When we reach this stage, we may become fearful of asserting ourselves, of taking control of our circumstances, and of acting on our own behalf.

Your mission, should you choose to accept it, is to gain an understanding of the fact that your loved one's misinformed and misguided efforts to control their emotions by controlling *your* actions does not help anyone, and therefore there is no reason for you to support their efforts. It may be unfamiliar, uncomfortable, even frightening, but you *can* take control of your life again.

Each type of relationship has its own set of criteria. In brief, if they are someone with whom you must have a relationship in order to have another, more important relationship, it is important to be supported, stay detached, use nondefensive communication, and refuse to be drawn into battle. An example of this would be a relationship with a daughter-in-law. Remember that relative sees you as a threat; your goal is to show her that people have an infinite capacity for love.

If your loved one is someone you expect to fill your needs, your challenge is to look at the situation the way it is—not the way it was or the way you would like it to be—and to give yourself permission to have your own needs. Your decisions must be based on reality, not fantasy.

If they are an abusive person from whom you need protection (or if you need to protect others), take this job very seriously. Do not rationalize any kind of verbal, emotional, physical, or sexual abuse. If children are involved, their safety comes first. They must make their own choices, and so must you. Make sure that your choice is the right one for the long term.

Reflection

After reading this chapter, what stands out to you?

_____

_____

_____

_____

_____

_____

_____

_____

_____

What have you learned in this chapter that you want to put into action?

_____

_____

_____

_____

_____

_____

_____

_____

_____

CHAPTER 10

Finding Qualified Professional Help

When I try to find help for my borderline wife, some clinicians tell me there is no such thing as BPD. I'd like to say, "'Why don't you spend a week with my wife?' Then I'd like to hear what you have to say."

—member of an online forum

Finding a clinician who is experienced in treating BPD or NPD is one of the most difficult issues HCPs and non-BPs encounter. People ask me for recommendations several times a week.

The problem is that, in essence, the clinician must help the person with BPD or NPD work through the anger, frozen grief, and other powerful emotions that are currently being directed your way. It takes a skilled person to set personal limits while being accessible, to help the HCP like themselves while motivating them to change, and to develop a close rapport without encouraging too much dependence. Clinicians are just like you in that they have triggers and personal feelings; they're just trained to deal with them.

First, Do No Harm

It can be difficult to find a clinician to work with BPD clients. At best, uninformed clinicians do not help. At worst, they make the situation worse, as one clinician who wishes to remain anonymous explained in an interview with me:

> One of my principal concerns is the absence of adequate training in the recognition and treatment of BPD, which results in bad outcomes for many. Most of my current clients ended up with me after multiple prior treatment failures, often because the therapist, while well-meaning, did more harm than good. Much of the damage occurs because the therapists have lousy boundaries, either because of their own issues or because they are inadequately trained.
>
> The "harm" results when the therapist recognizes the boundary violations and suddenly changes the rules, even blaming the BPD patient. Since issues of trust, rejection, and safety are so important to the BPD client, this therapist behavior can be very destructive.
>
> The second type of harm often occurs when patients requiring long-term treatment are invited into a short-term process, only to be dropped when money runs out. BPD patients need to understand what they are undertaking, up front. Most of the other problems occur via simple therapist incompetence.

Why Finding a Clinician Is Difficult

There are a number of reasons why it is hard to find professional help.

1.   Clinicians generally do not get enough training in personality disorders.

2.   Clinicians may have preconceived notions about personality-disordered patients in general.

3. People worldwide need help, and there is currently no international database of clinicians with expertise in treating personality disorders who are taking patients.

4. A clinician who may work well with one person may not develop a rapport with another. No credential or recommendation can guarantee a clinician's ability to help you or those you love.

5. People with personality disorders are some of the most difficult people to treat. Reiland (2002) describes beings so angry at her psychiatrist that she threatened a false sexual harassment complaint and once left a semi-threatening note on her psychiatrist's car. Two clinicians have personally told me of people with BPD who self-harmed during a counseling session and needed immediate medical treatment. Yet many clinicians find people with BPD some of the most rewarding people to treat; although therapy takes longer and is more difficult, the successes are all the more gratifying.

6. Psychology programs do not adequately train students for treating personality disorders, and a clinician may get just a few hours of training on BPD and NPD.

There are two kinds of issues in a therapeutic relationship: contractual issues and therapeutic issues. Contractual issues include things like appointment schedules, professional fees, and whether or not a given clinician has anything to offer you in resolving your problems. Therapeutic issues are those issues you talk about once the contractual issues are settled—your thoughts, feelings, actions, life circumstances, relationships, etc. Any worthwhile clinician will be very glad to hear you express your uneasy feelings about the therapeutic relationship. If they treat those uneasy feelings as though they represent something "wrong" with you, though, don't waste any more time on that clinician. Do not pass "Go" and do not collect $200—cut a trail right then, and look for another therapist. I know one individual who experienced exactly that sort of unease with a therapist, feeling vaguely that something was wrong but unable to put his finger on it, and later through his own research he discovered that the "professional" was not even licensed to practice.

Dialectical Behavior Therapy

DBT is also the only therapy that has treatment standards that stay the same from clinician to clinician. You can do a search on dialectical behavior therapy online. There are also books on the subject. The Behavioral Technology Transfer Group, Linehan's training organization, is in the process of posting an updated list of clinicians who have been through dialectical behavior therapy (DBT) training. Please refer to the clinical resource directory at: http://behavioraltech.com/find-a-therapist-app/.

Many clinicians, including those trained in DBT, are more familiar with treating low-functioning people with BPD or NPD who self-harm or who also have substance abuse or eating disorders. When interviewing clinicians, make sure they understand that high-functioning HCPs may not fit their stereotype of what a patient with BPD or NPD is like.

Reflection

After reading this chapter, what stands out to you?

_____

_____

_____

_____

_____

_____

_____

_____

_____

What have you learned in this chapter that you want to put into action?

_____

_____

_____

_____

_____

_____

_____

_____

_____

_____

Reading List and Resources

Resource Materials

Splitting: Protecting Yourself While Divorcing a Borderline or Narcissist (2011) by Bill Eddy and Randi Kreger

Bill Eddy specializes in representing clients divorcing someone with a high-conflict personality. This book offers the best advice and emotional support anywhere for those facing an emotionally wrenching, legally convoluted divorce. Eddy is also the author of *High Conflict Personalities: Understanding and Resolving Their Costly Disputes.*

The Splitting Companion CD (2007) by William A. Eddy

A lively discussion on two CDs with the author of *Splitting*, William A. Eddy (see previous book). He answers questions frequently asked by readers of his book and explains how a technique called the "assertive, balanced approach" can make divorcing a person with BPD a less harrowing experience for all and save thousands of dollars.

Online Family Support Groups

Moving Forward Online Family Support Group: https://groups.io/g/MovingForward

The Moving Forward online support group is a lifeline for individuals whose lives are affected by someone with BPD or NPD. It's a place where loved ones come for support, information, and understanding with others in their situation all over the world. Since I founded it in 1995, sixty thousand people have revolved through the community.

Books About BPD

Stop Walking on Eggshells: Taking Your Life Back When Someone You Care About Has Borderline Personality Disorder (2020) by R. Kreger and P. Mason, New Harbinger Publications

A self-help guide for family members and friends of individuals with borderline personality disorder. It helps them understand this self-destructive disorder and learn what they can do to help their loved one with BPD and themselves. It is considered the "bible" for family members and has sold more than a quarter million copies.

Stop Walking on Eggshells Workbook: Practical Strategies for Living with Someone Who Has Borderline Personality Disorder (2002) by R. Kreger, New Harbinger Publications

This book helps family members gain insight into their own role in the relationship. It also shows them how to navigate life with a person with BPD. It contains step-by-step suggestions for setting personal limits, communicating clearly, coping with put-downs and rage, developing a safety plan, and making realistic decisions. The book contains worksheets, checklists, and exercises that build on one another and enable readers to apply the suggestions to their lives.

Get Me Out of Here: My Recovery from Borderline Personality Disorder (2004) by R. Reiland, Hazelden Publishing

An accountant and mother of three, Reiland (not her real name) tells the poignant story of her life, which included all-too-familiar episodes of anorexia, promiscuity, impulsiveness, suicide attempts, institutionalization in a mental hospital, and behavior that was often unrelenting, anger-intensive, violent, and unpredictable. With astonishing honesty, Reiland reveals what having BPD feels like from the inside and how healing is possible through intensive therapy and the support of loved ones. Very hard to put down.

Skills Training Manual for Treating Borderline Personality Disorder (1993) by M. M. Linehan, PhD, Guilford Press

This workbook is intended for clinicians leading their patients in dialectical behavior therapy. However, laypeople can benefit from reading the book because it includes a large section of handouts and worksheets used in the skills-training portion of the therapy. These training sheets, designed to teach concrete skills, revolve around mindfulness, interpersonal effectiveness, emotional regulation, and distress tolerance.

Surviving a Borderline Parent: How to Heal Your Childhood Wounds and Build Trust, Boundaries, and Self-Esteem (2003) by K. Roth and F. Friedman, New Harbinger Publications

This book, the first written specifically for children of borderline parents, offers step-by-step guidance in understanding and overcoming the lasting effects of being raised by a person with this disorder. Learn what psychological criteria are necessary for a BPD diagnosis, and identify the specific characteristics your parent presents. Discover specific coping strategies for dealing with issues common to children of borderline parents: low self-esteem, lack of trust, guilt, and hypersensitivity. Make the major decision of whether to confront your parent about their condition.

Other Helpful Books

The books most popular with the Moving Forward community members are starred.

And I Don't Want to Live This Life (1996) by D. Spungen, Ballantine Books, New York

Better Boundaries: Owning and Treasuring Your Own Life (1998) by J. Black and G. Enns, New Harbinger Publications, Oakland, CA

Boundaries: Where You End and I Begin (1998) by A. Katherine, MJF Books, New York

Changing for Good (1994) by J. Prochaska, J. Norcross, and C. DiClemente, HarperCollins, New York

Children of the Self-Absorbed: A Grownup's Guide to Getting Over Narcissistic Parents (2001) by N. Brown, New Harbinger Publications, Oakland, CA

Choosing to Live: How to Defeat Suicide Through Cognitive Therapy (1996) by T. Ellis and C. Newman, New Harbinger Publications, Oakland, CA

Codependent No More: How to Stop Controlling Others and Start Caring for Yourself (1996) by M. Beattie, Harper and Row, New York

Controlling People: How to Recognize, Understand, and Deal with People Who Try to Control You (2002) by P. Evans, Adams Media Corporation, Avon, MA

Courtney Love, Queen of Noise (1996) by M. Rossi, Pocket Books, New York

Cutting: Understanding and Overcoming Self-Mutilation (1998) by S. Levenkron, W. W. Norton and Company, New York

* *The Dance of Anger, A Woman's Guide to Changing the Patterns of Relationships* (1997) by H. Lerner, Harper and Row, New York (also invaluable for men)

Diana in Search of Herself: Portrait of a Troubled Princess (2000) by B. Smith, New American Library, New York

Divorcing a Parent (1990) by B. Engel, Fawcett Columbine, New York

Don't Let Your Kids Kill You: A Guide for Parents of Drug and Alcohol Addicted Children (2005) by C. Rubin, New Century Publishers, Petaluma, CA

Don't Shoot the Dog (1999) by K. Pryor, Bantam Books, New York

Emotional Blackmail (1998) by S. Forward, Harper Paperbacks, New York

The Emotionally Abused Woman (1990) by B. Engel, Fawcett Columbine, New York

The Emotionally Abusive Relationship (2002) by B. Engel, John Wiley & Sons, Hoboken, NJ

Enough About You, Let's Talk About Me: How to Recognize and Manage the Narcissists in Your Life (2005) by L. Carter, Jossey-Bass, San Francisco

The Explosive Child (2002) by R. W. Greene, HarperCollins, New York

Feel the Fear and Do It Anyway (1987) by M. Rossi, Pocket Books, New York

Get Fit in Bed (2006) by G. Tartell and T. Kavanau, New Harbinger Publications, Oakland, CA

How I Stayed Alive When My Brain Was Trying to Kill Me (2005) by S. Rose Blauner, HarperCollins Publishers, New York

How to Change Anybody (2005) by D. J. Lieberman, St. Martin's Press, New York

How to Escape the No-Win Trap (2004) by B. Cowan Berg, McGraw-Hill, New York

How to Stop Worrying and Start Living (1944) by D. Carnegie, Pocket Books, New York

I Don't Have to Make Everything All Better (1995) by G. Lundberg and J. Lundberg, Penguin Putnam, New York

If You Had Controlling Parents (1998) by D. Neuharth, Cliff Street Books, Lewiston, NY

Is He Depressed or What? (2005) by D. B. Wexler, New Harbinger Publications, Oakland, CA

The Journey from Abandonment to Healing (2000) by S. Anderson, Berkley Publishing Group, New York

Loving Him Without Losing You (2000) by B. Engel, John Wiley & Sons, New York (appropriate for men, too)

Loving the Self-Absorbed (2003) by N. Brown, New Harbinger Publications, Oakland, CA

Neural Path Therapy: How to Change Your Brain's Response to Anger, Fear, Pain, and Desire (2005) by M. McKay and D. Harper, New Harbinger Publications, Oakland, CA

Perilous Rivalry: When Siblings Become Abusive (1991) by V. Wiehe and T. Herring, Lexington Books, Lanham, MD

Reinventing Your Life (1994) by J. Young and J. Klosko, Penguin Group, New York

Serenity to Go: Calming Techniques for Your Hectic Life (2001) by M. Hamilton, New Harbinger Publications, Oakland, CA

Stop Controlling Me! What to Do When Someone You Love Has Too Much Power Over You (2001) by R. Stenack, New Harbinger Publications, Oakland, CA

Teach Yourself Body Language (2003) by G. Wainwright, Hodder Education, London

Through the Eyes of Children: Healing Stories for Children of Divorce (1997) by J. Johnston, The Free Press, New York

* *Toxic Parents: Overcoming Their Hurtful Legacy and Reclaiming Your Life* (2002) by S. Forward and C. Buck, Bantam, New York

When Anger Hurts Your Kids: A Parent's Guide (1996) by P. Fanning, K. Paleg, D. Landis, and M. McKay, New Harbinger Publications, Oakland, CA

When Anger Hurts Your Relationship (2001) by K. Paleg and M. McKay, New Harbinger Publications, Oakland, CA

When Your Child Is Cutting (2006) by M. McVey-Noble, New Harbinger Publications, Oakland, CA

Other Online Resources

www.stopwalkingoneggshells.com

Randi Kreger, coauthor of *Stop Walking on Eggshells* and *Stop Walking on Eggshells Workbook*, maintains this site. Formerly known as BPDCentral, Stop Walking on Eggshells is one of the oldest, largest, and most popular sites about BPD on the web and offers an abundance of information about BPD for family members.

www.bpdrecovery.com/

BPD Recovery is for individuals with the disorder. It is a safe arena for those with BPD to share concerns, voice opinions, and seek like-minded people. It contains much information, a discussion board, and more.

www.bpdresourcecenter.org/

The BPD Resource Center is a nonprofit organization that provides reliable information on BPD and its treatment. It is associated with the New York Presbyterian Hospital, Westchester Division, in White Plains, New York. The toll-free phone number is 1-888-694-2273.

www.ContinuingEdCourses.net

An online course for mental health professionals titled "'It's All Your Fault!'–Working With High Conflict Personalities." The presenter is William A. Eddy, a nationally known attorney, therapist, and mediator. It is approved for ten continuing education credit hours.

www.nami.org

You can search for "borderline personality disorder" in the internal search engine on this page to find resources.

Organizations

National Education Alliance for Borderline Personality Disorder

http://www.borderlinepersonalitydisorder.org/

This organization, composed of some of the top clinicians in the United States, raises public awareness, provides education, promotes research on borderline personality disorder, and enhances the quality of life of individuals affected by BPD. It supports family education programs, hosts conferences, conducts family research, and publishes educational materials.

Personality Disorders Awareness Network

www.pdan.org/

PDAN is a nonprofit organization devoted to assisting family members of those with BPD, especially minor children affected by a parent's disorder.

Glossary

Abandonment, fear of. An unrealistically intense and overwhelming fear of being deserted and left alone, generally stemming from childhood beliefs that one cannot survive alone. One of the chief traits in someone with BPD, although it may be expressed in many different ways.

All or nothing. An attitude that reflects "splitting": seeing people or situations as all good or all bad.

Boundaries or personal limits. Reasonable expectations of how someone should expect others to treat them. People often learn how to treat you by seeing how you treat yourself, which is why it is essential to establish and observe your own boundaries. Some HCPs will push the limits to see how far they can go; if you anticipate and plan for this, it will be easier to observe your limits.

Codependence. You can find many different definitions of codependence, but most revolve around living your life with an excessive focus on the well-being of other people—especially if focusing on others causes one to neglect one's own well-being or personal limits. People who are codependent often need to be needed and are attracted to people they think they can "save" or change.

Cognitive behavioral therapy (CBT). A type of therapy that focuses on changing a person's irrational thoughts, which then will lead to different beliefs, resulting in changed behavior.

Cognitive distortion. Interpreting an event in a distorted way that leads to a faulty conclusion. They include: all-or-nothing thinking (splitting); overgeneralization (you weren't invited to the wedding so you assume everyone hates you); mental filter (focusing on a negative detail and missing the big picture, such as a mom with BPD complaining you're a terrible daughter because you forgot to call her); disqualifying the positive (one criticism outweighing an excellent performance review); "mind reading" without any other evidence (assuming their partner's bad mood is directed toward them when she had an argument with her boss); fortune-telling ("Why even try when I'll fail anyway?"); emotional reasoning (the belief that feelings equal facts); punishing themself when motivation is more in order (thinking "I'm such an awful fat slob because I ate that piece of cake," when they could think, "I ate too much today, but tomorrow I'll make better choices"); labeling (extreme overgeneralization of themselves, such as "I am a failure and always will be"); and personalization (taking full responsibility for an event when they may have just triggered it).

Consistency. Inconsistency is part of the human condition. We're not robots, and the same stimulus can bring on different reactions depending upon dozens of factors. But when you're interacting with an HCP, consistency—acting or reacting the same way every time— is the best way to effectively shape that person's behavior. Before you make a promise or threat, make sure you're prepared to carry it through.

Countermoves. A defensive response to change. If you begin to assert yourself, the HCP will find themself having to change, too. The HCP may then intensify the "unwanted" behavior or up the ante to see if your new boundaries are really serious. This is a critical time, for if you set a limit and go back on your word, the other person will learn you don't mean what you say.

Defense mechanisms. Common alternatives to uncomfortable emotions. They include suppression, repression, or denial of emotions, projection, sublimation (channeling emotions into an acceptable activity), and rationalization, etc.

Denial. A continual refusal to acknowledge clear facts, despite an abundance of solid evidence. Can be an initial step in the process of grieving (e.g., "forgetting" that a person has died and setting their place at the dinner table) or a continuing defense mechanism (e.g., "My father was great; he only beat me with his belt when I was bad and really needed it").

Dissociation. A feeling of unreality, or "spacing out," that characterizes BPD. Dissociation is not altogether an undesirable thing, depending on the particular form it takes. With BPD, dissociation serves the purpose of allowing the person to forget about extremely painful events, but it causes problems in relationships by causing the person with BPD to recall things very differently from the way they actually happened. Dissociation creates enormous confusion for someone in a relationship with a person with BPD, often causing them to wonder things like, "Am I going crazy?"

Emptiness. A chronic, painful emotional condition that drives much of BPD behavior. Often a person with BPD will use sex, spending, or some other impulsive behavior in an effort to fill an inner void.

Engulfment/abandonment. Two fears that are very common in BPD. When people with BPD fear "engulfment," they fear that someone emotionally close will "take over" their personality (since they feel their own identity is so tenuous). So they move away from the other person—picking a fight, for example. Fear of abandonment is the other side of the coin: an intense fear of being deserted and left alone. These two fears operate in BPD to create a push-pull situation in which the person with borderline does not want another person to get too close, but at the same time does not want them to get too far away (I hate you—don't leave me). A non-BP often experiences these twin fears as being simultaneously pushed away and pulled closer.

Enmeshment. An intense emotional bond with another person that is so pervasive it can seem that you lose your identity in the other person—some people describe it as not knowing where one person ends and the other begins. A feeling of being "lost" unless in the immediate company of the other person is an example of enmeshment. Both non-BPs and people with BPD can become enmeshed in each other to the detriment of both.

FOG. An acronym for Fear, Obligation, and Guilt, three potent weapons of emotional blackmail.

Gaslighting. Taken from the old movie *Gaslight,* this tactic is a process of trying to make someone doubt their sanity enough to believe they are "crazy."

High-functioning. With respect to BPD, this term refers to the people with BPD who are able to hold down jobs, maintain social relationships, and generally appear to be perfectly healthy. This may be possible because the struggles with intimacy, abandonment, and other painful emotions are only triggered by people the person with BPD feels close to and thus has something to lose. Non-BPs in relationships with high-functioning people with BPD usually need a great deal of validation since only they may witness the person's confusing or hurtful behavior. High-functioning people with borderline rarely seek therapy (they don't think they need it). If you are reading this book and relate to the material, you probably know a high-functioning person with BPD.

Hoovering. Doing everything imaginable to pull somebody back into a relationship after they have backed away; it often feels like getting "sucked" back in, as if by a vacuum cleaner.

Hypervigilance. An ongoing condition of guardedness, generally more so than a situation realistically calls for. A habit of staying on "red alert." In this context, it may include things like being very "jumpy" and overreacting to sudden movements and noises in ways that other people do not react. Often a component of post-traumatic stress disorder.

"I" statements. A way of communicating about yourself by beginning your statements with the word "I." "I" statements are useful as a means of avoiding a defensive reaction. Where BPD is concerned, making "I" statements is an important skill to learn because BPD can cause someone to be extremely thin-skinned and sensitive to criticism, whether the criticism is intended or not.

Impulsivity. Doing something out of immediate desire without adequately looking at the realistic facts or consequences of a situation.

Integrity. Everyone has a moral code—values that guide us daily. We develop these values from a combination of many things: the way we were raised, our religious beliefs, what experience has taught us, and so forth. People who act with integrity treat themselves with love and respect. People who compromise their integrity—say by not returning the money when they know they were undercharged, or letting people cross their personal limits—may rationalize their behavior (i.e., "I'll do this just this one time") or change their values. In the long run, not honoring your integrity leads to a loss of self-respect. Even if no one else is aware of your actions, you are.

Invalidation. Invalidation is giving someone the spoken or unspoken message that their feelings, personal experiences, or point of view is wrong, or not valid. Telling someone "You're too old to want to be hugged" or "Boys don't cry" is an example of invalidating someone's feelings (of grief or needing intimacy). Invalidation can also be a pattern of denying someone else's sense of reality (e.g. saying, "I'm cold, so go put on a sweater").

Over time, the invalidated person receives the message, "Something is wrong with me," or "I can't be trusted to take care of myself." People with BPD, who may have been raised in an invalidating environment themselves, often consciously or unconsciously use invalidation to convince non-BPs that the person with BPD is "right" and they are "wrong."

The key for non-BPs to get off this hamster wheel of confusion and depression is to get validation from other supportive people, validate themselves, and learn to acknowledge statements (so the person with BPD feels heard) without necessarily agreeing with them. It's also vital to accept that often there is no one "truth" and the person with BPD has a right to their point of view; and if the person with BPD has the right to their own opinion, so does everyone else—including you.

To be validated is to feel understood. To a twelve-year-old girl, being ignored by the popular crowd is a crushing blow. A father might validate her feelings by sympathizing with his daughter and showing that he understands what it means to her. If he tells her not to feel bad because she is young and will have friends later in life, he is invalidating her feelings (even if what he says is true). Validation is not about "truth," it is about acknowledging another person's feelings. Some researchers believe that an invalidating environment can contribute to the development of BPD.

Low-functioning. With respect to BPD, this term refers to someone who engages in self-harm or other extreme behavior that makes it easy for other people to recognize the presence of mental or emotional illness. Low-functioning people with BPD may be frequently hospitalized, on disability, and have severe eating disorders or engage in substance abuse. Non-BPs who have low-functioning people with BPD in their lives are usually not as isolated, invalidated, and confused as non-BPs with high-functioning people with BPD because it is apparent that their loved one has problems.

But they have other worries and fears since the person with BPD can seem so emotionally fragile and dependent on them.

Non-borderline, or non-BP. The term "non-borderline" (non-BP) does not mean "a person who doesn't have BPD," even though some people use it this way. Rather, it is shorthand for "relative, partner, friend, or other individual who is affected by the behavior of someone with BPD." Non-BPs can be in any type of relationship with someone who has BPD. Non-BPs we interviewed were married partners, unmarried partners, friends, children, parents, siblings, children-in-law, aunts, uncles, cousins, and coworkers of people with BPD. Non-BPs are a diverse group of people who are affected by people with BPD in a variety of ways. Some non-BPs are very supportive of people with BPD in their lives; some may be verbally or physically abusive. Non-BPs may have mental health concerns of their own, such as depression, substance abuse, Attention Deficit Disorder (ADD), and borderline personality disorder. People with BPD are also considered non-BPs if they are coping with someone in their life who also has BPD.

Observing personal limits. Acting in a manner that is respectful of another person's wishes. For example, observing personal limits is being on time as opposed to keeping another person waiting.

Personality disorder. A more entrenched "state" disorder that involves a person's way of dealing with life vs. a "trait" disorder (like depression) that is more transient and not an integral part of a person's makeup. These disorders are listed in the *DSM-V* (APA 2022).

Post-traumatic stress disorder (PTSD). This disorder can result from repeated and continued exposure to traumatic attacks. Traits include hypervigilance, recurrent and intrusive distressing recollections of the traumatic events, efforts to avoid thoughts, feelings, or conversations associated with the trauma, inability to recall an important aspect of the trauma, difficulty falling or staying asleep, difficulty concentrating, and an exaggerated response to being startled. The disturbance causes clinically significant distress or impairment in social, occupational, or other important areas of functioning.

Rages. Outbursts of anger that are a common occurrence in BPD. They may be triggered by some event, or they may seem to come out of thin air.

Reality checks. Everyone has their own version of "reality." If you ask each member of a couple why they broke up, for example, you will probably get two different stories. Someone who has BPD, however, can be extremely forceful about their reality, whether it's about your negative traits or a request that feels like manipulation (but you're not sure). Before you accept anything that doesn't "feel" right, do a reality check by getting input from friends who are willing to be truthful, won't feel put in the middle, and whom you believe to be mentally healthy.

Safety plan. A concrete, specific plan to avoid harm to the person with BPD, yourself, and/or minors during a period when someone with BPD is acting out in ways that feel threatening to yourself or other family members.

Self-harm, self-mutilation. Self-injury is a coping mechanism that low-functioning people with BPD use to release or manage overwhelming emotional pain—usually feelings of shame, anger, sadness, and abandonment. It is *not* a suicide attempt—in fact, it can be a way of feeling more alive, less numb, and less empty. Reasons for self-harm vary: They include self-punishment, to feel more "real," to communicate emotional pain to others, or to ask for help. Not all people who self-harm have BPD, and not every person with BPD self-harms. Unfortunately, many clinicians do not know this because they only see people who come in for therapy. *Stop Walking on Eggshells* (Mason and Kreger 2020) suggests ways to cope with self-harm.

Splitting. According to BPD researcher Marsha Linehan, PhD (1993), "Borderline individuals frequently vacillate between rigidly held yet contradictory points of view. They tend to see reality in polarized versions of 'either/or' rather than 'all,' and within a very fixed frame of reference. For example, it is not uncommon for such individuals to believe that the smallest fault makes it impossible for a person to be 'good' inside. Such thinking among borderline individuals has been labeled 'splitting' . . . Victims of childhood abuse conceptualize responsibility for their abuse in black-and-white terms. Either their abusers were all bad for abusing them, or they were all bad because they were abused. This is 'splitting' in psychoanalytic terms" (35).

Stigma. An extremely negative label. Many mental health practitioners avoid making a diagnosis of borderline personality disorder because it carries a strong stigma with insurance providers and even other mental health practitioners.

Suicide. About ten percent of people with borderline personality disorder eventually commit suicide. Suicide threats should always be taken seriously.

Testing. Disrespecting a person's stated personal limits to see if they will be observed; testing of limits is typical behavior in children and some adolescents. It is also common among adults with BPD. When someone tests your limits, your actions speak louder than words. If you let someone overstep your limits, they will continue to do so no matter what you say. Therefore, make sure you are serious about what your limits are before you set them.

Trigger. An event, action, smell, phrase, or something else that reminds you of a past experience and brings on a cascade of emotions. For example, if you and a former lover had a song you considered "your song," hearing that tune ten years after the end of the relationship (even if it's Muzak, unfortunately) may evoke strong, familiar associations (thoughts, memories, and emotions) with that romance. As a non-BP, you may inadvertently "trigger" the person with BPD and vice versa. When the association is positive, things go along smoothly. But if the association is negative—for example, a reminder of a profound loss—you may find yourself on the negative receiving end of something you won't understand.

Validating environment. An environment in which one is given the message that their thoughts, feelings, and personal experiences are "okay." Non-BPs find that they need friends to provide a validating environment during times when the person with BPD accuses them of any number of things—usually feelings and behaviors projected onto the non-BP. Marsha Linehan (1993) theorizes that BPD may be partly caused by an "invalidating environment"—that is, the person was told that their feelings were "wrong." As a parent, it may help to acknowledge a child's feelings, whether or not you consider them "justified" or "normal."

Validation. A universal human need to be believed and valued, given credibility, and acknowledged. Through the process of validation, you begin to feel real, grounded, and worthwhile. Without validation, you can actually feel "crazy," especially if you know something is real and people whose opinions matter to you disagree with you.

APPENDIX C

Safety Plan for Domestic Violence Situations

If you are experiencing domestic abuse, it is vital that you put together a safety plan. Use the following checklist so that you are prepared to leave.

☐ Prepare an "emergency kit" in the event that you need to leave quickly. An emergency kit should include copies of the following: important documents such as lease agreements or house deeds; birth certificates; your life insurance policy; medical and dental insurance cards; school records for children residing with you; Social Security cards; and bank statements. Also take your ATM cards, checkbook, credit cards, benefits card, loan payment books, mortgage coupons or rent receipts, protective orders, divorce or separation agreements, and medical records. If you can, take important membership IDs, photos, and your driver's license, vehicle insurance, and title and registration information. The kit should also include cash.

☐ Identify possible escape routes from various locations in your home. Determine their accessibility should you need them in an emergency. Doors, windows, staircases, elevators, and fire escapes are all possible escapes if you are being attacked.

☐ Keep an extra set of car and house keys in a convenient but secret location. Check this location occasionally to be sure the keys have not been taken.

☐ Give children, family members, neighbors, and friends a signal or code word for notifying the police should you need help. Make sure that children know how to dial 911, can provide the address of your home, and can give directions if necessary.

☐ Open a savings account in your name only. Have any records of it from the bank sent to the address of a trusted friend or family member. Put in a regular amount each month. *Having your own money is essential.*

☐ Whenever possible, don't allow arguments to start in confined areas such as bathrooms, hallways, stairwells, or areas where dangerous instruments are located, such as the kitchen, garage, or workshop of your home.

☐ It is *vital* that you keep notebook with a log of all abuse: what was done, who said what, and who may have witnessed the abuse. Document any violence and anything that points to your loved one's disorder such as therapy bills, hospitalizations, and false calls to 911. Keep a copy of all official documents, such as orders of protection, there as well. Your log should be kept in a place where the HCP cannot find it but you have access if you must leave immediately

References

Altınok, A., and N. Kılıç. 2020. "Exploring the Associations Between Narcissism, Intentions Towards Infidelity, and Relationship Satisfaction: Attachment Styles as a Moderator." *PLOS One 15*, no. 11: e0242277.

American Psychiatric Association. 2022. *Diagnostic and Statistical Manual of Mental Disorders (DSM-V)*. Washington, D.C.: American Psychiatric Association.

Black, J., and G. Enns. 1998. *Better Boundaries: Owning and Treasuring Your Own Life*. Oakland, CA: New Harbinger Publications.

Driessen, M., J. Herrmann, K. Stahl, M. Zwaan, S. Meier, H. Hill, M. Osterheider, and P. Petersen. 2000. "Magnetic Resonance Imagine Volumes of the Hippocampus and the Amygdala in Women with Borderline Personality Disorder and Early Traumatization." *Archives of General Psychiatry* 57, no. 12: 1115.

Engel, B. 1990. *The Emotionally Abused Woman: Overcoming Destructive Patterns and Reclaiming Yourself*. New York: Fawcett Columbine.

Engel, B. 2000. *Loving Him Without Losing You: Seven Empowering Strategies for Better Relationships*. New York: John Wiley and Sons.

Fjelstad, M. 2013. *Stop Caretaking the Borderline or Narcissist: How to End the Drama and Get on with Life*. New York: Rowman and Little-field.

Forward, S., and D. Frazier. 1997. *Emotional Blackmail: When the People in Your Life Use Fear, Obligation, and Guilt to Manipulate You*. New York: HarperCollins.

Hamilton, M. 2001. *Serenity to Go: Calming Techniques for Your Hectic Life*. Oakland, CA: New Harbinger Publications.

Lawson, C.A. 2000. *Understanding the Borderline Mother: Helping Her Children Transcend the Intense, Unpredictable, and Volatile Relationship*. Northvale, NJ: Jason Aronson, Inc.

Linehan, M. M. 1993. *Skills Training Manual for Treating Borderline Personality Disorder*. New York: Guilford Press.

Linehan, M. M. 2015. *DBT Skills Training Handouts and Worksheets*. 2nd ed. New York: Guilford Press.

Lobel, D. S. 2018. *When Your Daughter Has BPD: Essential Skills to Help Families Manage Borderline Personality Disorder*. Oakland, CA: New Harbinger Publications.

Mason, P., and R. Kreger. 2020. *Stop Walking on Eggshells*. Oakland, CA: New Harbinger Publications.

Preston, J. 2001. *Lift Your Mood Now: Simple Things You Can Do to Beat the Blues*. Oakland, CA: New Harbinger Publications.

Reiland, R. 2002. *I'm Not Supposed to Be Here: My Recovery from Borderline Personality Disorder*. Milwaukee, WI: Eggshells Press.

Roth, K. 2004. *Surviving a Borderline Parent: How to Heal Your Childhood Wounds* and *Build Trust, Boundaries, and Self Esteem*. Oakland, CA: New Harbinger Publications.

Selby, E.A., and T. E. Joiner. 2009. "Cascades of Emotion: The Emergence of Borderline Personality Disorder from Emotional and Behavioral Dysregulation." *Review of General Psychology* 13, no. 3: 219.

Whitbourne, S.L. 2021. "How Emotions Go Downhill in People with Personality Disorders." *Psychology Today*. September 21, 2021.

Randi Kreger is coauthor of *Stop Walking on Eggshells*, and author or coauthor of three other books: *The Stop Walking on Eggshells Workbook, The Essential Family Guide to Borderline Personality Disorder,* and *Stop Walking on Eggshells for Parents*. Kreger is owner and moderator of the "Moving Forward" family support group, which can be accessed at her website: www.stopwalkingoneggshells.com. She has given presentations throughout the United States and in Japan. She also has a one-on-one coaching practice which can be accessed through her website.

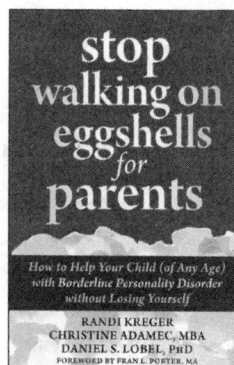